ACTON'S MUSIC

Photograph: Pat Langan.

ACTON'S MUSIC

Reviews of Dublin's Musical Life
1955–1985

Edited by Gareth Cox

KILBRIDE BOOKS

First published in 1996 by Kilbride Books
14 Rosslyn, Bray, Co. Wicklow, Ireland.
Telephone +353-1-286 3996   Fax+353-1-286 4349

Copyright © Gareth Cox, 1996
All rights reserved.

ISBN 0 948018 32 1

Apart from any fair dealing for the purposes of research or private study, or criticism or review, as permitted under the Copyright, Designs and Patents Act, 1988, this publication may not be reproduced or utilised in any form or by any means, electronic or mechanical, including photocopying and recording, or by any information storage and retrieval system without permission in writing from the publishers.

Design and production by Ted & Ursula O'Brien, Oben Design
Typesetting by Oben Design in 11pt *ITC Giovanni*
Index compiled by Oula Jones
The Editor is grateful to *The Irish Times* for its co-operation
Reproduction of Photographs by Colour Repro Ltd
Printing by ColourBooks Ltd

CONTENTS

Foreword By John O'Conor	7
Introduction	9
A Critic's Creed	15
Reviews, 1955–1957	31
Interlude — Acton In Bayreuth	48
Reviews, 1960–1965	53
Interlude — Why Drag In The Anthem?	77
Reviews, 1966–1967	80
Interval — Correspondence	93
Reviews, 1967–1971	105
Interlude — Eurovision Song Contest	120
Reviews, 1971–1981	122
Interlude — The National Concert Hall Saga	151
Reviews, 1981–1985	162
Index	181

FOREWORD

Charles Acton is sorely missed. It is now over nine years since he retired as music critic of *The Irish Times* and even his most implacable foes would wish him back where he reigned for so long. Of course he could be infuriating and perplexing at times but there is nobody who can match his experience, enthusiasm, compassion and exuberance.

The musical life of Dublin was his passion and also that of his wife Carol who was always by his side. It was he who fought for the establishment of the National Concert Hall, for concerts to begin on time, for promoters to provide English translations of the words at Lieder recitals and for a thousand other causes too.

He attended hundreds of concerts each year from the lowliest student performances to gala evenings with world stars, and treated all with the same dignity and respect. He nurtured promising young Irish talent and his encouragement and high standards contributed greatly to the present situation where there are more Irish performers and composers visible on the world's stages than ever before.

His reviews could be devastating at times but if a performance touched his soul the joy and infectious warmth of his love of music flowed from his pen. I wonder if we will ever be fortunate enough to find his like again.

John O'Conor
January 1996

Charles Acton receiving the first Seán O'Boyle Award from Mrs Alice O'Boyle at the United Arts Club in Dublin. 1986. (Photograph by Jack McManus)

INTRODUCTION

> If there is one single person who over the last quarter century or so has bestrode the musical scene in Ireland like the proverbial Colossus, that individual has been Charles Acton. Courted and accommodated by the musical profession while at the same time feared and maligned, he remained the critic that the public never chose to ignore.
> (Michael Dervan, *The Irish Times*, 1/10/86)

Charles Acton (or "C.A." as he was first known), was senior music critic of *The Irish Times* from 1955-1986. He was born, coincidentally, in Iron Acton near Bristol on the 25th of April, 1914, into a family that can be traced back to the 12th century, and with an estate (until 1944) at Kilmacurragh, Co. Wicklow. His father, a major in the British Army, fell at Ypres in 1916. Following family tradition, he was educated at Rugby where he learned to play the bassoon, an instrument he was to play in the Dublin Orchestral Players in the 1940s and 50s. (Although a keen amateur pianist, his sole public appearance as a pianist was in the German Institute in 1968 in a performance (!) of John Cage's silent piece, *4' 33"*). At a school concert in Rugby he enjoyed what he describes as the marvellous experience of hearing the City of Birmingham Symphony Orchestra under Adrian Boult playing Brahms's *Academic Festival Overture* and conducting the whole school in the singing of *Gaudeamus igitur* with the orchestra. He also cites hearing Elgar conducting *The Dream of Gerontius* at the Three Choirs Festival in 1932 in Worcester Cathedral, and Toscanini conducting all the Beethoven symphonies with the BBC Symphony Orchestra in London in 1935 as other memorable musical experiences of his youth.

He read Natural Sciences (physics, chemistry and mineralogy) at Trinity College, Cambridge, although he was more interested in the theatre and writing music reviews with Brian Boydell for *Varsity Weekly* than taking a degree, one of his reviews being of the première of Vaughan Williams's *The Poisoned Kiss*. As a student he spent the summer of 1935 in Munich where he heard Richard Strauss conducting *Elektra, Die Frau ohne Schatten, Salome, Josephs-Legende* and *Der Rosenkavalier* and Hans Knappertsbusch conducting *Lohengrin, Tannhäuser, Parsifal*, and the entire *Ring* cycle. He left Cambridge in 1936 having failed his degree and went to work as a booking clerk for Thomas Cook in London and, from 1937, in Palestine, where he subsequently ran a small library.

He returned to Ireland in 1939 and embarked on a series of jobs with varying degrees of success: as a farmer, as a barman in a hotel, manufacturing charcoal during the war years for running cars, lorries and Post and Telegraph vans, and as a salesman for the *Encyclopaedia Britannica* and Proctor's Tripod Harvesting Ltd. In 1951, he married Carol Little, violin teacher at the Royal Irish Academy of Music, leader of the Dublin Orchestral Players and later a successful music journalist in her own right.

Acton himself describes the lucky break which proved decisive for his future career:

> At the Wexford Festival of 1955, my immediate predecessor, Dr A. J. Potter, had certain problems which

have passed into Wexford folklore and had also told our then Editor what he could do about it. The first rule of motoring is "Don't drive into a Garda car". So, a contributor's first rule must always be "Don't tell the Editor what he can he do about it." Accordingly, Jack White, then Features and Literary Editor of the paper (and to whom I owe more than I can ever describe), rang Joseph Groocock to ask him to become the paper's music critic. Joe turned the idea down flat, but, to my lifelong gratitude, suggested asking me. And that is how it started.

(*The Irish Times*, 7/11/80)

Acton began slowly, often only earning around £8 a month in his first year, but in the next 31 years, he was to review over 6,000 concerts employing a conversational and eminently readable style; from very fine concerts: *this performance which I saw through a haze of tears and emotion while hearing a wonderful experience*, to very bad: *I emerged from the RDS last night boiling with anger at a grievous insult offered to Beethoven's genius.*

His reviews were written for a deadline of 11.30 p.m., but he always preferred this to the continental practice of publishing reviews a few days after the concert because, as he says, *if you don't do it straight away the steam has gone out of it and you ask yourself, "Did I really enjoy this concert so much?", or "was it really as bad as that?" and soften it a little until it comes out pretty neutral.* This meant that he could rarely stay for encores, but he felt strongly that encores should not be reviewed anyway, his theory being *that the critic should write about the programme that is offered to the public for money even though the performer has encores that he regards as part of the evening.* He recalls that he had *a nice row with Jimmy Galway on the subject because he was so annoyed with my going out immediately before the encores, that for one concert he only published the first half of his programme and said the second half would be encores, so, all right, I left at the interval.* Despite differences of opinion and many unfavourable reviews over the years, he is proud of the fact that he did not lose many friends, although he admits that *they might have been a little distant the next time you met them.* He always found that between the sincere critic and the truly professional performer of merit there was a relationship of mutual, professional respect.

Gerard Victory, composer and ex-Director of Music in RTÉ, stated that Acton's "vision of a hoped-for ideal musical world in Ireland was fiercely intense [and] when this vision did not come to pass at the pace he would have wished his impatience and chagrin could frequently blaze forth from his column." Apart from castigating audience behaviour at a time when it was not unknown for popcorn and chocolates to be eaten during concert performances at the Theatre Royal, and when inconsequential coughing was rampant, he campaigned unceasingly for a National Concert Hall, adequate Arts Council funding, stressed the importance of a standardised and punctual starting time for concerts (managing to get the now-standard time of 8.00 accepted), and attacked RTÉ continually in print for what he considered to be a shirking of its national and institutional responsibilities to Irish artists, composers, concert-goers, and radio and television audiences. On Acton's 75th birthday, his successor Michael Dervan succinctly characterised his particularly discursive rhetoric: "Polemics seem to come easily to Charles. His views are so strongly held, and the strands of his polemics so closely interwoven, that it wasn't unusual for single concerts to provoke a torrent of deeply-felt commentary that wasn't always directly related to the music on the programme or the performances on the night. Although performers may from time to time have been dismayed at the outcome, the uniquely personal tone and the unmistakable throb of heartfelt concern were what made these diatribes such compulsive reading."

Apart from reviews, Acton also wrote major articles on practically every subject of musical interest in Ireland such as RTÉ, the Concert Hall, Irish traditional music (in connection with which he received the first Seán O'Boyle award in 1986), the Feis Ceoil, the Music Association of Ireland, the Dublin Grand Opera Society, the Wexford Opera Festival, music facilities, the Arts Council, Irish composers and music education. He also contributed regular record reviews (which he often used as a general musical sounding-off to the extent that discophiles would sometimes plaintively wonder when he was actually going to review the records), articles previewing the week ahead, annual reviews, interviews with visiting composers and artists such as Olivier Messiaen, Andrzej Panufnik or Yehudi Menuhin, obituaries, portraits, as well as finding time for the occasional "Table for Two" and to contribute articles to journals such as *Feasta*, *Éire-Ireland* and *The Musical Times*. In 1978 Easons published his *Irish Music and Musicians* as no. 15 in their "Irish Heritage Series" and he also wrote a short study of Irish pianists from John Field to the present day for the programme of the first GPA Dublin International Piano Competition. In the Gate Theatre, Dublin in 1974, he expounded his personal tenets of music criticism in a talk entitled *A Critic's Creed*, which is published here for the first time.

Charles Acton retired officially in 1987 and the following year presented his entire collection of concert programmes to the National Library: this "Acton Collection" constitutes a unique and valuable historical source for future documentation of this period. In 1990 he was elected a Fellow of the Royal Irish Academy of Music.

Many people have hoped that Acton would write a book

of memoirs about the period of musical life in Ireland that he was so much a part of. In the absence of such a book, this compilation of reviews aims to recall for concert-goers past and present some of the outstanding musical events in Dublin during the period 1955-1985, as reflected in his reviews. Selecting a mere 65 reviews from the 6,000 that Acton wrote was obviously an extremely subjective task and the collection regrettably omits the enormous contribution made to Dublin's rich and varied musical life by countless foreign and Irish artists, choral societies, orchestras and ensembles.

Gareth Cox
Limerick, 1996

A CRITIC'S CREED

A TALK BY CHARLES ACTON,
The Gate Theatre, 20.10.74

EVERY now and then a critic is attacked from various directions for what he has written. This is as it should be. It is his function to sit in judgment on others, and it would be neither fair nor natural for others to refrain from judging him. If he is prepared to comment on the doings of other people (although by their invitation and on his Editor's instructions), it is only right that he should try to act responsibly, be ready at all times to defend his opinion; and be ready to retract or apologise if he finds himself factually in the wrong. On the other hand the critics of critics often attack on quite the wrong grounds, and it may be useful to set out the critical creed of one critic, in one journal. Let us be clear about this. Like all criticism, even this is a personal statement of belief about his responsibility by one individual. His colleagues may have different (and equally valid) creeds. Therefore let us move into the first person, and grant as a premise that we are concerned with criticism of music in Dublin, Ireland, in *The Irish Times*, by Charles Acton, and with its practice rather than its aesthetics.

Criticism is opinion; the opinion of one person only. That is always true: it is especially true when it is signed — though that could lead to a long digression. It is usually compatible with, or sympathetic with, the general personality of the journal in which it appears; not by any command or persuasion, but in the nature of things. That is as far as it goes, because no Editor worth his salt interferes with a critic, whom he has sufficient confidence to retain, save very rarely to guide him and help him to better criticism. Even more, no Editor worth his salt will countenance economic or political interference to secure a good notice or to withdraw a condemnatory one. (In parenthesis, I beg this opportunity to thank the Editors of *The Irish Times* for their unfailing loyalty, support and understanding help, which I know to have been given me even at times when my firmly held and firmly expressed opinions have brought all sorts of hornets buzzing into their office.)

Criticism remains one person's own personal opinion — however expressed. One of my colleagues makes a point of principle of never using the first personal pronoun. This policy is maintained consistently, but that does not deny personalism of view. It has been said that every critical notice should be headed "In my opinion..." To try to make this invisible first line mentally visible, I (unlike my colleague) make a point of putting at least one "I" into every notice and of putting an "I" near any adverse opinion which is arguable. This practice leaves one open to the retorts "Who cares what you think?". and "Just what is your opinion worth anyway?" The answer to the first is "anyone who honours me by reading this" — for all my apparently self-opinionated writing, I do feel humbly awed by the appreciation of so many readers. The short answer to the second question has been given once and for all by Frank Howes of *The Times* of London: "Fourpence tomorrow morning". Egotistical as such criticism may sound, it has been a matter of amusement to me that, on almost every occasion when I have omitted to insert "I" into a notice, some idiot has written to the long-suffering Editor to say that my views were not necessarily shared by all the audience. Heaven forbid that they should be!

That criticism is an expression of an identifiable individual's opinion means that it is subject to the whole corpus of that individual's outlook on music (and life, perhaps), all his likes and dislikes. He tries to brush these aside, but no one can really get outside his personality. I do not like Mascagni or Menotti: I believe my dislike to be reasonable and defensible; but it is there, and my readers who like these two composers will be aware of the fact of my dislike. This means that the critic's opinion should not be judged on a single notice, and is part of the relationship between him and his readers. It may be hard on the visiting artist who, naturally, only sees the single notice out of its matrix: that cannot be helped. It is also hard on the friends and relations of the local artist who only buy *The Irish Times* when dear little Mary has given a recital of gems from Menotti. Even less can that be helped, since *The Irish Times* is an excellent paper and they should read it every day.

But that brings us to the order of the Irish critic's responsibilities, using the word in all its senses. And it is fair to say here that this talk owes not a little to the aftermath of an unscripted discussion on Radio Éireann with this title that took place under Brian Boydell's chairmanship in which I appeared then as a mere member of the musical public.

The critic's first responsibility, by a very long way, is to his readers. He is writing, first and foremost, for those who read his paper. That does not mean that he must temper his views to fit in with the paper's policy or his idea of his readers' prejudices. It does mean that, for *The Irish Times*, neither the tabloid style of the *Daily Mirror* nor the intense, avant-garde scholarship of *The Score* is suitable. On the other hand, there is no reason why his readers should always (or even usually) agree with him. If he can stimulate his readers to do their own thinking and yet make them feel that his views are on the whole worth considering, fair and reasonable, he is doing a great deal of his proper job. This matter of continuity and balance is important. Again and again, I have been amused to find that people who are kind enough to tell me they respect and approve of my criticism are up in arms when exactly the same treatment is applied to the concerts they are personally interested in. On the whole, far too many people lack a self-critical capacity.

Perhaps an Irish music critic's prime responsibility is (in theory) the advancement of the practice and enjoyment of the art in Ireland. In fact this must always come second to his responsibility to his readers, but there is not in fact any conflict. This brings us straight away to a question of standards. There is a school of criticism (supported by a predecessor of mine) that there is only one standard of judgment — the highest. He would have one judge the performances of the RÉSO by the standard of the Vienna Philharmonic Orchestra and castigate them when they are below those standards. I believe that idea to be utterly wrong, impracticable and harmful. It is ridiculous to expect the RÉSO in a dozen years to achieve the level of an orchestra with a century and a half's tradition of being Europe's leading orchestra. To do so is to be blind to the facts of life and, worse, is to discourage everyone concerned. But more of encouragement later. Furthermore such a policy inevitably means that almost every notice is a matter of carping, cavilling and castigation. An unpleasant critic is an impossible one, and a bore to his readers, however accurate his judgments. And, again, however valid such a standard might be in London, Paris, Vienna, New York or San Francisco, it is invalid in Dublin, or in any capital of a musically small country.

I believe that one has to set a standard for each type of

event and consider how the actual example compares with that standard. That of course brings us back to continuity, because one cannot in practice define one's standard in every notice. Reader and writer must agree to a lot by inference and custom. I believe that (broadly speaking) the standard of judgment should be what the particular performer is capable of, tempered by whether that is proper to the reader's attention. Thus, a performance in a student concert may rightly be described as outstanding if it is so in the context of Dublin student concerts. To say so is not to suggest that the student is as good as Paderewski or would necessarily be a bright light of the Juilliard Conservatoire. Such differences of standards of judgment are implicit in all regular criticism. Another field for them is that I try to keep a more rigorous standard for foreign performers than for Irish. If a foreign artist is to take the trouble to come here, to offer his wares outside his own community and take our Irish money, he should be worth it. There is no earthly point in importing Britons, Germans, Americans or Italians unless they can give us something we should not get without them. That is no matter of xenophobia, of protection of inefficient home talent. It is straightforward common sense that the Irish artists of sufficient merit should be able to expect support from Irish audiences and Irish critics. Thank goodness we do get a wonderful range of performance from all sorts of nations, but we certainly have at least two Irish organisations presenting concerts who sometimes seem to think that all British geese are swans, and Irish swans all geese. It is part of the critic's responsibility to the public and to the Irish performer to offer a watchful balance and to hold it in favour of our own.

These particular considerations do not, of course, apply to the world's front-ranking artists. They have something to give to any community, but equally it is an impertinence to judge them by any but the very highest standards. And if they have not declined from this highest level that is what they appreciate. Virtually all accomplished artists are perfectly well aware of imperfection in their performance. Incidentally, performers, if they are any good, know far more about what went wrong than any critic - never mind what the critic writes. Their managers may be pleased by mere adulation; they themselves will respect an informed judgment more than mere adulation. ("I never look at notices" is as flagrantly untrue of musicians as of actors). When fixing standards, circumstances must be weighed. We are right to judge a pianist at the RDS more rigorously than a string quartet. There are scores of pianists for every one quartet; quartet playing is a more difficult art than pianism; there are fairly few quartets that the RDS can afford.

There are of course occasions when the critic must raise his standards abruptly and most of his regular readers know that he is doing it and why. Such an occasion is the Dublin Music Festival. The standards by which one judges Phoenix Hall or RDS events are not suitable for an International Music Festival. The latter is only justifiable if its standards of performance and musical interest are on the level of Edinburgh, Salzburg or the Maggio Musicale. Broadly speaking, I believe that an Irish critic should judge each event by what he believes to be the best that is practicable in the circumstances; that he should demand that foreigners should justify their importation; that he should try to keep a sense of scale from the VPO [Vienna Philharmonic Orchestra] to the village band.

I believe that the critic should keep before himself and his readers the great truth, that *Music is meant to be enjoyed*. Poor music poorly performed cannot give satisfaction or real enjoyment. The obverse of asking foreigners to justify themselves is to have no truck with the treasonable idea (apparently rife in revivalist circles) that it is enough for a thing to be Irish, no matter how bad. Music can only flourish here or anywhere else if the public is prepared to buy tickets for it and the critic does a disservice to the public (and therefore the performer) if he condones what is patently and unnecessarily unenjoyable. Some otherwise intelligent musicians tell me that I should only praise. "After all the practice and time and hard work and spiritual energy the artist has put into it, should not the critic only praise the good things and not point out to the ignorant public the various defects? Furthermore the poor fellow will get discouraged after all his effort". Put crudely this amounts to the old request: "Don't shoot the pianist. He is doing his best". Encouragement is a different matter that must be considered later.

Now, let me suggest that a performer in real danger of discouragement from a responsible critic would do better to take up another trade or at least not to invite the public. After all, it is in the performer's hands, or at least his promoter's, whether there is a critic present or not. The critic goes only because he is invited: and cannot write a notice if he is not invited. (As a corollary, of course, the paper might feel obliged to state that its critic had not been invited if the question ever arose). Nevertheless this well-meaning, charitable outlook ignores two very important points. The readers of this newspaper are paying for my honest judgment, within the context of the event. To mention only the good things would be breaking faith with the readers. (There are, of course, a certain number of events where one must resort to the mealy-mouthed compliment and conceal the truth. Readers of average intelligence can and do read between the lines of such notices). The other point is that where there is nothing but praise the praise loses its meaning entirely. We all know the sort of laudatory, local-paper notice that leaves the intelligent reader no wiser but for the suspicion that the performance was dire. If I rave about Isaac Stern (as I did), that has no meaning at all if I use the same sort of expressions about little Mary Cassidy who has been unwise enough to offer herself as a celebrity in the Theatre Royal. On the other hand if I maintain a reasonable balance, then my rave means a great deal. (That can be discovered to work also in reverse). A relevant point that often escapes both the performers and the supporters of this charitable school of (no-) thought, is that somebody is usually asking the public to pay good money (or its equivalent) for the pleasure of hearing the event.

The critic may fairly take the secondary responsibility to the future of the art as one of his readers' ideals also. An Irishman who believes that music is one of the graces of life, part of the whole person's spiritual fulfilments, must hope that the majority of his fellow citizens will eventually come to take pleasure from private music making and public concerts; that the music in his country shall be as good as in anyone else's (*ceteris paribus*); and that Irish professional musicians of good standard may practise their profession, earn their livings and enjoy public approbation in their own country. It is from this that arises any responsibility he may have to performers, composers, organisers; and such responsibilities are secondary and derivative. And any such responsibility must be exercised within the primary ones. And the critic must try to blend the experience of the present with the hopes of the future.

Here we come to the question of encouragement. Let us presume at the moment that we are talking about past, present or would-be professional performers (we adopt different standards for amateurs). I believe that it is part of an Irish critic's function to encourage these Irish artists to persevere — when they are good enough — and to encourage his readers to go to listen to them. But such encouragement must only encourage the good and the worth while. Encouragement of the third rate by excessive kindness and not enough adverse comment is a long-term cruelty. Not long ago a London colleague at the end of a very firm notice wrote: "I strongly recommend Miss —— to return home and consider matrimony instead of music". Brutal? Seemingly! But far, far kinder than the terrible callous cruelty of the public, each of whose silent words is an empty seat.

Let us look at this question of encouragement, of critic-performer relationship: In the 1951 Feis Ceoil, little Mary Cassidy won the under-9 Ophikleid Class with a remarkably good performance for her age. She therefore featured as the star of my notice of the Feis Junior Prizewinners' concert — how glad the critic is for something really good at these occasions! In subsequent years up to 1957, say, notices of Feis concerts and RIAM Student Union Guest Nights contain various glowing accounts, for there is no doubt that Mary has great talent. In 1955, perhaps, I had to warn her about an incipient vibrato: In 1957 I had to remind her against burying her undoubted musicianship under her remarkable technique — even Popof's "Toccata-Fantasy on Yesteryear" has a little music in it. In 1958 Miss Mary Cassidy played Khachaturian's Ophikleid Concerto at the Phoenix Hall, prior to her departure to study with Dr Wurstfagott in Austria. I found that this promising young player gave a very mature performance of this extremely difficult work and wished her every success in her foreign studies. In 1960 she gave a solo recital at one of the MAI's coming-out recitals. Undoubtedly she has made further progress, is definitely a promising young Irish artist and gave us a good deal of pleasure. But, in view of her new status and the "Wigmore Hall" purpose of the MAI's coming-out recitals, I am bound to point out that she was not quite ready for coming out, that her unaccompanied Bach (it is remarkable what J.S.B. wrote for!)

lacked complete conviction and she did not seem to understand the full significance of the Boulez piece. In 1962 she will return, now 22 years old, and give another recital, this time under her own auspices. She will have then reached the beginning of those two, three, four or five terrible, cruel, brutal years when she is trying to climb onto the list of accepted ophikleid soloists. In these years, she will discover, the hard way, whether her name will be in lights, or even whether she can earn a living as an ophikleidist of any sort. Now she will get no quarter from the public, the agents, the managements or the critics. Now she is no longer the "promising young Irish artist": now she is master of her art or nothing. Luck, stamina, guts will all play their part: And if she deserves it, praise from an impartial critic can help her. But only if she deserves it. She is now beyond all mere encouragement, utterly on her own in her bitter struggle. If she has no hope the critic is kinder to tell her so. You, the kindly, soft-spoken public, who want me to pull my punches, will starve her remorselessly by not wanting to pay out hard-earned money to go to listen to her. It is as simple as that.

In the field of this secondary responsibility, I believe that the critic should encourage the performance of Irish works. Composers depend upon performance. Dr Larchet, with a most dignified humility, referred on Radio Éireann to "that great Irish composer for whom we are all waiting and hoping". He will not arise unless Irish composers' works are performed. Not only must composers live on performances, but only by performance can they learn their trade. A critic should goad concert organisers to use Irish composers, he should goad composers into composing. We should welcome all new work wherever from, but he is entitled to adapt to this situation Sir Thomas Beecham's remark about British appointments: "Why import all these third-rate foreign conductors when we have plenty of second-rate British ones?" But again the critic is forced to see to it that poor stuff is castigated and to try to assess Irish composition truthfully. He will be abdicating his responsibility to his readers — and to the composers — if he merely praises the bad indiscriminately — and there must be so much bad.

In his magnificent article on criticism in his *Oxford Companion to Music*, Scholes denies that the critic has any responsibility to the impresario. I disagree. I believe he has the same secondary responsibility as to the composer or performer. After all, it is the impresario, management, organiser (whatever one calls it) that engages the artist, decides the programme (within the artist's then repertoire) and invites the public's attendance. The enjoyment of the music is affected by the hall being too cold or too hot, distractions of movement or noise, late starting or other deficiencies. Apart from that, the policy of organisers is of vital public interest, since very few artists are their own sponsors.

By now, perhaps, I have established a general creed of one critic in one paper in Ireland. A few typical comments and instances may fill in the body of the picture. There is the controversial question of comparing one artist with another. All criticism rests on comparison — that is how standards are made. As a matter of courtesy and convention, one usually avoids comparing live artists of similar stature — although one does in gramophone records, poems and other arts. One may compare them (favourably or unfavourably) with the dead, but not with each other. This convention is thoroughly practical and useful, even though one's readers are busy making the comparisons that the critic avoids. But there are, I believe, exceptions. If one management is so foolish as to offer us two 18th century oboe concertos by two soloists in 48 hours, it is unrealistic to ignore the fact. Again, if three Dublin concert organisations bring three international pianists within three weeks and have them all play Chopin's Berceuse and F minor Fantasy, it is ludicrous to shut one's eyes to the fact. For a critic is writing continuously for a continuous audience. He must assume that his readers (as a corporate entity) are equally interested in all events as a continuity of Dublin music. If the artist does not like it, he must blame his impresario, not the critic.

I believe that the critic should emphasise the community of music. He should encourage audiences to mix: he should deplore any tendency for the RDS audience not to go to the opera; for opera audiences to keep out of the Phoenix Hall; for the followers of one choir to avoid the concerts of another choir; and so on. Such exclusiveness harms music.

Some readers think that critics should be masters and virtuosos of each genre upon which they comment. Apart from the sheer impracticality of any paper retaining a regiment of different music critics, it is desirable that a critic can see the wood as well as the trees. Also there is the question of continuity already referred to, the inadequacy of Wagner as a critic of Brahms, vice versa and a whole range of similar incompatibles. Perhaps Dr Johnson settled this one finally when he said: "You may abuse a tragedy, though you cannot write one; You may scold a carpenter who has made a bad table, though you cannot make one. It is not your trade to make tables."

Considering the trouble some organisations go to to tell the critics about their stars' careers and triumphs elsewhere, it is surprising how remiss they are in not telling him of stray circumstances that may affect the performance. If a singer has a cold or has just heard shocking news, I should be told. Not that I should overlook a bad performance; but so that I can either tell the readers, or so phrase my remarks that both truth and humanity are served. This is really important. We in the audience are often totally unaware how professional performers are loyally and wonderfully fulfilling their engagements in circumstances that would prostrate the rest of us. Here are three examples: I once castigated the machine-like performance of a conductor. I did not know that his wife had died the day before [Charles Munch with the Boston Symphony Orchestra in 1956]. I once condemned the poor performance of a famous pianist at the RDS. And it was a poor performance. The RDS could easily have told me, what I only learnt a year later, that she was appearing in two recitals in one day within seven days of a serious miscarriage. I have damned an opera singer, only to learn later that I had in fact heard the understudy and she with a heavy cold. Three gross and unwitting unkindnesses, so easily prevented. In no case would I have praised the performances had I known, but the artists and my readers would have received a much fairer idea. It has been said that a critic must speak for the cash customer who has paid his money. Perhaps, but full information enables him to do justice to all and injustice to none.

One reads of the venality and corruption of the music critics of 19th century Paris and Italy. A few jaundiced people imagine that here in Dublin we get together to concoct unfair notices. (These are of course the same people who protest when critics very properly differ). It is in fact a matter of great satisfaction that Dublin criticism is completely honest, Whatever may be wrong with it, neither venality nor conspiracy are. If you see critics together, as you often do, you may take it that their conversation is roughly the same as yours. A facet of this problem is that of acquaintance with the people concerned. The London critic, Scott Goddard, said that he is so much afraid of acquaintance influencing opinion that he makes a point of not being acquainted with any performer. This abnegation is perfectly practical in London — with a little effort. In a community of Dublin's size it could only be achieved by firm and resolute determination to hold no musical conversation, to take part in no music and censor one's social contacts most carefully. Were such an attempt successful, I believe that it would lead to a certain inhumanity and to a serious ignorance of our hopes and trends and possibilities — which brings us back to standards.

On the other hand, I firmly believe that it is possible to be on terms of acquaintance and even friendship with the subjects of one's criticism without either the criticism or the friendship suffering. I would go further than that. A critic's influence is not only between himself and his readers. It may be small, but there is a certain amount that passes by way of oral suggestion that smooths the presentation of future events and gets better programmes or material arrangement for the public. This may be very small, but it has mounted up in the long run. And it often means that the critic can thereby avoid putting cavils into notices, even though the things badly need saying. For it must be remembered that one of the critic's objects in a notice is to produce a balance of praise or blame that in reading corresponds to his total impression. It is too easy to write of an enjoyable concert full of good and beautiful playing and then to devote the rest of the notice to the defects. Similarly to start off referring to a dull, boring and tedious evening of bad music badly done, and then spend 200 words fishing up the few good details. The reader will end by regarding the first as a damning and the second as a laudatory notice.

That brings us to three things that are difficult. Firstly, to praise adequately the very good to the length of a notice. Defects of performance are where the performer departs from the composer's intentions (or what the critic believes these to be). It is easy to point to differences. Really good performance implies identity of performer with composer.

Comment then approaches programme note.

Secondly, to deal with the nondescript concert, where there is little demonstrably wrong, except for that spark of communication. And especially when the performer is an established local artist of little importance, of no possibility of improvement. Excoriation will achieve nothing — anyway it would be out of place: the necessary dose of faint praise can too easily look like real praise, the more so in comparison with the third difficult thing. This is the really good performance that deserves detailed analysis of the few points, change or improvement of which would achieve greatness. Serious and helpful discussion of these is worth while and important. And yet such discussion, space consuming as it is, can make a whole notice seem far less favourable than something more crabbed of a less important concert. This is almost a critic's largest problem.

Perhaps the largest problem of all — or at least his greatest anxiety — is the fear of injustice and unfairness arising from his own mood. A gas meter is a constant and accurate measurer of gas. The critic is a human being. However hard he tries it is almost impossible to divorce his particular state of mind, health or emotion completely from the opinion he expresses. He tries his level best to make allowance for any such disturbances, to be as judicial, constant, unchanging as possible; but he is well aware that he is very fallible. Nonetheless, while only too well aware of fallibility and frequent inadequacy, I still believe that the critic who tries to be responsible to his paper's readers, to interest them, to help them to enjoy more music and who tries to help performers and the general improvement of music in Ireland, is a small stage of an important process that can over the years make Ireland a good place for her citizens to live, and an honoured corner of a civilised world.

Charles Acton receiving honorary life membership of the National Union of Journalists at the Clarence Hotel, Dublin, from Paddy Clancy, chairman of Dublin Freelance branch. September 1987. (Photograph by Tony Galvin)

REVIEWS
1955–1985

SEGOVIA'S RECITAL IN THEATRE ROYAL

Segovia, the master of the guitar, delighted the large audience in the Theatre Royal, Dublin, on Saturday afternoon. In this theatre the largest orchestras rarely can give the listeners more than a mezzo-forte: Yet, strangely, this simple slight instrument could be heard right at the back. But, of course, a cough was a loud noise, and an outburst of coughing during the playing of Albeniz's *Torre bermeja* seemed to disconcert Segovia himself as well as the listeners. And it was presumably the gale of cold air that he had to endure on the stage that accounted for the feeling that he was a bit tired just before the interval.

In Segovia's hand the guitar looks so easy! And what a great range of tone it has: as it were, the registration of a harpsichord or small organ. With this subtlety of tone and dynamics Segovia can pluck his strings for two hours without the slightest monotony. But of all the separate items a few seemed to stand out especially — V. Galileo's little pieces for lute (how delicate they are, quite apart from the historical curiosity that he was the astronomer's father); the complex varieties of rhythm of Bach's contemporary, Weiss; the Prelude, Fugue and Gavotte of Bach himself; Villa-Lobos's complicated and moving Etudes, and Castelnuovo-Tedesco's surprisingly gentle Tarantella.

28th November, 1955

MESSIAH SUNG AT TCD

At the performance of Messiah by the University of Dublin Choral Society in the Examination Hall of Trinity College,

Dublin, last night, the choir itself stole the show, which is quite proper. That they knew whose was the responsibility for that was shown by their own and the audience's tumultuous applause for Joseph Groocock, their conductor.

It apparently is the society's excellent policy that each generation of students should have one opportunity of singing *Messiah* which accounts for their doing it — they ought to include the B minor Mass in this routine too. But, as one would expect in a university and of Mr Groocock, this was no routine performance. Of the making of versions of Handel there is no end: the one used was published probably during Handel's lifetime; but there will never be a definitive version on account of Handel's habit of using whatever resources were available for each performance and filling in *ex tempore* on the organ. Last night's version was suitable in that it was a possible reconstruction according to the limited resources available.

This particularly applies to the orchestra (led by Barbara Barklie) and the piano continuo by Alicia Turnbull. The players did well, but it is shocking that the university cannot raise more than about four undergraduate players — is this another consequence of there being no live faculty of music? In principle, it was a good thing to replace the difficult trumpet by the far easier cornets — but what a pity that the Trumpet Shall Sound so sharp.

For all but seasoned whole-time professionals the well-known arias must be a terrifying ordeal, and all the soloists suffered to some extent from nerves, except Norman Myers (bass) who took it all in his stride. Olwen Roe's contralto voice is pleasant and well produced, but much too small for the part. Ralph Walker (tenor) sang well, but should speed up his recitatives: by taking them so slowly he lost the dramatic effect of slowness and dragged the whole work. Best of all was Dorothy Hall (soprano) who soon recovered from her nervousness and sang her half of "He shall feed His flock" very beautifully.

To return to the choir. They were obviously at one with the conductor, and fired by his enthusiasm and ideals. They sang very well in tune, giving great dynamic contrasts, and with great verve and intelligence. There seem to be no passengers here and what a pleasure to hear such good tenors and basses, usually a weakness in Dublin choirs!

Again, it was the choir's evening — and that means Joseph Groocock's.

7th December, 1955

CONTRASTS IN PERFORMANCE BY BOSTON SYMPHONY ORCHESTRA

Symphony no. 102 in B flat — Haydn
Elegy in Memory of Serge Koussevitzky, op. 44 — Howard Hanson
Tone Poem, Don Juan, op. 20 — Richard Strauss
Symphony no. 2 in C, op. 61 — Schumann

I really enjoyed and was moved by the last couple of minutes (from the last pause) of Don Juan on Saturday at the Theatre Royal, Dublin; and by some expressive playing in the Adagio of the Schumann symphony. In these two passages the Boston Symphony Orchestra showed some life and feeling. But the rest of the afternoon was essentially a demonstration of what is probably the most efficient musical machine that we have heard here.

When the BBC Symphony Orchestra came in April they proved to be very slick indeed, but with little soul. One hoped that this was merely a stage in Sargent's development of them and that he will eventually get the machine to make real music. The Boston orchestra proved to be even slicker, with virtually no soul. Charles Munch has now been with them for seven years and he should have been able in that time to get from them the feeling and poetry of music as well as technical perfection. After all, technique is but the means, and not the end of expression.

This was the third time this year we have had *Don Juan* in Ireland. Our own radio orchestra has no pretensions to being a world-famous top-flight body, but, in all seriousness, its playing of *Don Juan* was much more enjoyable than Saturday's, because it was alive, had feeling and was done with zest. And that was but a shadow of the Vienna Philharmonic Orchestra's playing in Cork in May.†

Obviously the blame must rest largely with Charles Munch, the Boston's conductor, but does it go deeper than that?* In forging this machine, have the players forgotten to enjoy the making of music as such? Except for some of the woodwind (especially the first flute) it seemed very doubtful if any of the players really got a kick out of playing their music.

Perhaps they also felt that it was not a very exciting programme. It was such a pity that with major modern American music so unknown on this side of the Atlantic, they should not have brought us something really interesting and memorable. Howard Hanson's Elegy proved to be a highly academic piece of *fin-de-siècle* romanticism, but not worth bringing three thousand miles to represent the music of the U.S.A.

All this seems very harsh and ungrateful after we have been accorded the opportunity of hearing in our own capital one of the world's famous orchestras. It is probable that in Boston their performances are wonderful; that Saturday was one of those off-days that all artists have. But one can only judge what one hears. And it is because of their fame and position that they have the right to be judged by the highest standards and asked to come back again and play from the heart — to add feeling to precision, exhilaration to technique. As it was on Saturday, they committed the one great sin against the spirit of music — they were boring. This was so sad after all the fanfares of publicity among the panoply of Church and State, and made one feel all the more bitter that in May the Vienna Philharmonic were not accorded a welcome in our capital as they were in Cork and Limerick.

27th August, 1956

† The VPO also performed Beethoven's Symphony no. 7, Weber's *Euryanthe* Overture and Mozart's Symphony no. 40, K. 550. They only played in Cork and Limerick and Acton reports that, had the train to Cork crashed, Dublin would have lost most of its musicians.

* See also *A Critic's Creed* p. 27 and *INTERVAL* p. 93.

LIBERACE AT THE THEATRE ROYAL

In the middle of his performance at the Theatre Royal, Dublin, on Saturday afternoon, Liberace complained about English music critics. It was surprising that he should be so thin-skinned. To judge by what we read, he landed in England as a combination of Liszt, Beethoven, Duke Ellington, visiting royalty and Billy Graham. He went to the Royal Festival Hall instead of to the London Palladium. The music critics (rather than the theatre critics) were invited to hear the keyboard marvel of the age. They found a first-class variety entertainer, and objected to having been misled.

At the Theatre Royal, he met a sceptical audience waiting with interest, but no particular enthusiasm, to see what would happen. They had read their newspapers: they had read their programmes (which implied that he was an outstanding serious artist). Then the performance started, and they politely applauded and chuckled at the appearance of each of the famous phenomena — item George, item the silk suit, item "Mom", item the electric candelabrum. He had to work extremely hard to win his audience. By hard work, and a really well done act, slickly and expertly put together, he did win them triumphantly.

As he has said himself, Liberace is not a concert artist, but an entertainer. All the glitter, the gold, the smile and the charm are part of the well-planned act, and fit in as well as any stage décor. His commentary and general attitude were refreshingly honest — he makes us laugh *with* him at the preposterous glittering clothes, at his blatant advertising of his records.

In Palm Court, in commercial jazz and the Sydney Smith type of display, Liberace is an extremely fine player with a beautiful technique. In his few serious works his playing was without much merit. Why do so many variety stars try to convince us that they can perform straight, great music?

One cannot object to his combining Gounod's *Ave Maria* with Schubert's into a cloying mass of notes — it is what each of these maudlin pieces has been asking for for a century. But his pot-pourri of gems of Chopin did show us that we are lucky to have so little of this sort of music.

Most top-of-the-bill variety artists confine their appearances to the strategic points in the programmes. Liberace is on the stage virtually all the time in the 2-hour programme and he is certainly versatile: his talk, his ready wit, his singing (if you like that sort of thing), his dancing, are all of a piece with his light-hearted playing. George deserves all the applause he got: he is an accomplished violinist, and he can get plenty of sparkle out of our normally rather sedate RÉ Light Orchestra. On the other hand, the very unobtrusive Gordon Robinson (arranger, fill-in pianist, spare conductor, and probably almost everything else as well) deserves the applause that he avoids.

As Liberace gradually won his audience to enthusiastic pleasure, I found myself wondering whether there can ever be a bridge between the showmanship and sparkle that goes with this light music, and our enjoyment of serious music which we usually take so very solemnly. I am not asking for Solomon in sequins; but is there a half-way house?

15th October, 1956

DIE WALKÜRE AT THE GAIETY

Anyone is a fool who wilfully misses the Essen Opera's *Walküre* which had its first performance at the Gaiety Theatre, Dublin, last night. It is twenty years since I last saw the opera, and I had thought that I was permanently cured of the Wagner fever. But last night the magic was there with all its overwhelming power. If this notice is disjointed, that is because I have not yet recovered.

Wagner's protagonist is, of course, the orchestra. Radio Éireann's brass is so unreliable that I had been dreading what it would do in a night of Wagner. But throughout the first act they were excellent: they declined later, but they could never break the spell wholly — the stage electrician very nearly succeeded sometimes; perhaps he will be more efficient in the other performances.

To return to the orchestra, Gustav König, as a conductor, made it do wonders, and the bite and attack of the lower strings in particular were thrilling. The sets and costumes by Alfred Siercke are an admirable half-way stage between the tedious old-fashioned tradition and Wieland Wagner's remarkable Bayreuth essays — as also was the production by Hans Hartleb, which avoided the static and the over-athletic.

Last night's six principals were splendidly even, none perhaps among the giants (except Wotan), but none ineffective. Wotan was Herbert Flitscher. He has a rich, round, pure, sonorous voice that made every note, every phrase, expressive and musical. His performance was extremely fine and moving, so much that his farewell to Brünnhilde, and "So küss' ich die Gottheit von Dir" brought me completely to tears.

But the heavy brass should be boiled in oil for so execrably ruining that tremendous statement of the *Vertragsmotiv* immediately following. Though he is not a great *Heldentenor*, Günther Treptow was a pleasing Siegmund; Paula Brivkalne an excellent Sieglinde; and the splendour of Xavier Waibel's singing made Hunding's early disappearance a pity. I would say that Tilla Brien has not a forceful enough voice for Brünnhilde, but she was so moving in the last act that I hardly have the heart to say so. Trude Roesler was an admirable Fricka.

I am really grateful to the Dublin Grand Opera Society for giving me this really memorable experience. Please, if you possibly can, go and revel in it also.

28th November, 1956

BILL HALEY AND HIS COMETS

When the high priest of rock 'n' roll, Bill Haley with his Comets, opened at the Theatre Royal, Dublin, last night for the first of a series of four concerts, somebody cynically remarked that 75% of a capacity audience had gone there out of curiosity to see how the remaining 25% of the aficionados would react. They certainly saw one of the most remarkable displays of audience participation ever seen in this city and I feel that at the end of the show the disparity was no longer 75% — 25%. Some converts must have been made along the line to this strange, exciting and infectious new rhythm. Rock 'n' roll quite obviously is not music, but it is a new-style rhythm which cannot be ignored and should stay with us a little while longer. There is no doubt whatever that in this department — to adopt the language of the "cats" — Bill Haley and his extremely talented sextette is "the most".

Each "Comet" is a musician in his own right. Franny Beecher, for instance, has long been recognised as one of the top Spanish electric guitar players. He has played with several renowned groups, including both Benny Goodman's famous Sextette and his big band — and that does not just happen by accident. Beecher last night was right at the top of his form, and so was Billy Williamson, the steel guitarist, Al Rex (bass), *et al.* Bill Haley's 40-minute programme was almost completely rock 'n' roll; but it was the established favourites — his "good luck" tune, "Rock Around the Clock", "See You Later, Alligator" and "Shake, Rattle and Roll" — which really whipped his young audience to a vivid frenzy of enthusiasm.

The balance of the programme was supplied by Vic Lewis and his Orchestra, a finely balanced band of musicians, whose playing at times was not treated too kindly by the theatre's system of amplification, and a section of the current week's variety programme (which I think nobody really wanted very much). It was Haley's night, and beside him everything else paled into insignificance.

1st March, 1957

BAMBERGER SYMPHONIKER

Overture, Euryanthe — Weber
Symphony, Mathis der Maler — Hindemith
Symphony no. 3 in E flat, op. 55, "Eroica" — Beethoven

I hope those who disagreed with me about the Boston Orchestra were at the Theatre Royal, Dublin, on Saturday afternoon to hear the Bamberg Symphony Orchestra. For here was an orchestra that had not got that hard, machine-made perfect precision of the Boston, but which had all that feeling for the music that the Boston seemed to lack. What a Beethovenesque performance of the Eroica! Every note, every marking seemed to be felt and appreciated as Beethoven wrote it. What moving, taut expressive playing of the strings in the Funeral March!

The same love and feeling for the music informed both the overture and the Hindemith. I am suffering from a growing conviction that Hindemith is, after all, a somewhat barren composer and that his *Mathis der Maler* is too bitty and fails to achieve effects of sonority worth the large resources employed. But I must admit that on Saturday the work was very much more thrilling than when our own orchestra played it at the Gaiety, although the seat I was given, tucked away behind the violas and basses, was not the best to listen from (I moved elsewhere for the Beethoven). And the final brass chords were really thrilling, particularly with the clean, level, crisp tone of the Bamberg trumpets.

May I interpolate two complaints here? Firstly, this concert seemed to be very inadequately publicised — hence the sadly sparse audience. Secondly, the too-expensive programme should surely have told us the name of the admirable leader, something of the orchestra's remarkable history, and not assumed that we are part of Britain.

I have left to the end Joseph Keilberth, the conductor, so as to finish with praise for so much of the afternoon's pleasure. He is probably the best conductor we have seen here for a considerable time. In every movement (or absence of movement) can be seen a deeply sensitive musician who can completely communicate his feelings. He and the orchestra are clearly at one. In performance he has no need of display to impress the audience, nor of fuss to secure ensemble — they play together almost as chamber music players, and his frequent periods of immobility show how perfectly they do so. His conducting and the orchestra seemed concerned to bring us the essence and the spirit of the music, so that this concert was a really memorable event.

25th March, 1957

MENUHIN CONCERT IN THEATRE ROYAL

Overture, Egmont op. 84 — Beethoven
Violin Concerto in D, op. 61 — Beethoven
Adagio for Strings — Samuel Barber
Violin Concerto in E minor, op. 64 — Mendelssohn

Robert Magidoff's biography had filled me with an extreme expectant interest in Yehudi Menuhin's appearance with the

Philharmonia Orchestra on Saturday afternoon in the Theatre Royal, Dublin, and I could not but keep the book in mind when assessing his performance.

But before that main business, two grouses about the programme. The extreme poignant beauty of the Barber Adagio is too intense to put between Menuhin's performance of these two concertos. We could not take it: hence it was almost drowned by coughing. (Oddly enough, those coughers never coughed during either concerto). Something jolly and vulgar would have eased the tension, such as Sibelius' Karelia March.

Secondly, without detracting from the thrill of the Mendelssohn, when we have a violinist of this calibre, how splendid it would be to pair the Beethoven with a great modern concerto, the Bartók or the Bloch!

The Orchestra's role was secondary, so I shall only refer here to its beautiful woodwind playing, and the stodginess of Egmont due to Efrem Kürtz's rather jerky and pedestrian conducting.

Menuhin's playing was a very great experience. Gone was the apparently uncaring pyrotechnician of his last visit to us. One could no longer say (as a critic once did) that he has a glorious future behind him. Here was a great artist.

The same qualities were revealed in both concertos, so I shall use the Beethoven as the text. There were faults in plenty. His intonation was very variable: the tone of the cadenzas was surprisingly hard: there were bits of the first movement that were almost dull. But just as I was beginning to get disgruntled, the first few bars after the cadenza were a beauty. Again, the rondo started very solidly: but then it started dancing, and all was well.

If in the outside movements the glory was veiled, the middle movement showed forth the supreme artist. This was the Menuhin for whom we have hoped and waited so long.

It would seem that his personal crisis as an artist, as a player, is not yet wholly passed; that he is still only emerging from it.

It is now impossible to doubt his sincerity as a musician: He played that Beethoven from the inside; with a passionate understanding and inwardness. This was not just performance, just display; it was the revelation of great music.

My over-all impression is of a superlative artist, violinist, musician who is still finding himself, at the dawning of a new fruitful period. He is yet a young man for all that he has experienced, and I think we may look forward to a glory greater than we have known.

20th May, 1957

BARBIROLLI'S MEMORABLE *GERONTIUS*

Ten minutes after the advertised time of starting, Sir John Barbirolli was still standing watching the late-comers take their seats yesterday afternoon at the Theatre Royal, Dublin, before the performance of *The Dream of Gerontius*. This discourtesy was all the more marked by the fact that Sir John was obviously conducting in considerable pain, and everyone who was present must pay tribute to him for coming in spite of his accident.*

In the event, Sir John and Our Lady's Choral Society made this performance memorable. If this was a replica of their performance in Berlin last year, no wonder that that was received so rapturously. After Sir John himself, the stars were the choir. The evil of the demons; the roof-lifting "Praise", the flowing line and delicate detail of "Lord Thou hast been"; their whole performance was better than I have ever heard either in this work, or from them. A great deal of credit must go to their chorus-master, Oliver O'Brien.

Similarly, the Radio Éireann Symphony Orchestra[†] played as they rarely have before — in all sections — and gave every nuance that Elgar or Barbirolli required. It is a lift to our spirits that they can play like this — when will it be their habit? But what a pity they were not all in front of the proscenium arch (as the Royal Ballet orchestra was), so that the full bloom of their tone could have come to us.

I cannot be quite so enthusiastic over the three soloists. True, Ronald Dowd's Gerontius was nearly all I wanted, but he seemed to lack poignancy and sweat of agony — but that may have been the fault of the building. In a performance of this level, one thinks of other Angels — Ferrier, Desmond, Marjorie Thomas — and I found that Constance Shacklock did not give us the continuity of flow that her music needs. It was a good performance, but not a great one. Similarly, Marian Novakowski's is not the voice I would have chosen for the part of Priest or Angel of the Agony, but within those limits he gave of his best.

But I do not mean to carp. Barbirolli's reading, and what he got from choir and orchestra, made a performance of this great work that can seldom have been equalled.

10th June, 1957

[*] Barbirolli had fallen off his rostrum in Manchester and seriously hurt his back.

[†] The RÉSO was to become the RTÉSO and in 1990 the National Symphony Orchestra (NSO)

THE MARRIAGE OF FIGARO

I am thoroughly delighted that the knives I had sharpened in anticipation of the Dublin Grand Opera Society's *Marriage of Figaro* had to be sheathed unused at the Gaiety Theatre last night. Mozart should not be done unless really well, and after all the storms and arguments of the last few weeks* I must confess that I did not expect "Figaro" to satisfy me. But no one at the Gaiety can have enjoyed himself more than I did — not even my neighbour who greeted the overture with "How I love the music," and talked through it and most of the first act.

Before letting loose the superlatives, I must record three disappointments. For me Anne Bollinger spoilt an otherwise very intelligent performance of the Countess by having the wrong sort of vibrato. The Countess can do a lot of other things wrong provided the first four notes of "Dove sono" are the purest sound on earth. Secondly, James Pease delighted me throughout in every way except that he would not really let himself go in "Non piu andrai" — it must be really rumbustious. Thirdly, though the chorus were an admirable collection of skivvies and scullions, it would have been nice to hear them — fortunately they occupy a very minor place.

Now for some of the good things. Howell Glynne's Doctor Bartolo was a delicious buffo and Barbara Howitt's Marcellina was as wholly excellent as had been her so different Niklaus in *The Tales of Hoffmann*. In their several ways Martin Dempsey (Antonio), Margaret Nisbett (Barbarina), Kevin Miller (Basilio), Niven Miller (Curzio) were equally excellent.

Geraint Evans as the Count gave me absolutely everything I wanted from him. Patricia Kerm's Cherubino was a sheer delight. This part is so often either ineffective or embarrassing, but Miss Kerm's performance was wholly convincing throughout: I shall long remember her eyes as she sat in the chair; and her singing matched the rest of her performance — particularly "Voi che sapete".

And now Susanna herself. During the whole evening I completely lost my heart to Adèle Leigh. I leave her last as the one who gave me greatest pleasure. At the moment, I do not believe there could be a better Susanna.

All this joy surely came about because the whole thing was an intelligently conceived unity. The constructivist scenery by Christopher West and Jennifer Agnew was just what the DGOS should aim at more often. Christopher West had achieved some sophisticated and yet really comic production. Bryan Balkwill made the RÉSO play real Mozart and (my congratulations) *never* drowned the stage.

This just shows what the DGOS can do when it put its mind to it. If only this were their *regular* standard — and surely it could be. But is it not unfortunate that this masterly performance can only be seen twice more — on Saturday and Tuesday next? Finally, how vastly greater the music (and the music drama) of Mozart is than that of Offenbach, Puccini or Gounod.

6th December, 1957

* Contentious correspondence comparing the DGOS with Wexford Opera had appeared in the "letters page".

INTERLUDE

Charles Acton attended and reviewed many European festivals and cultural events such as Edinburgh, Verona, Glyndebourne, Aix-en-Provence and Prague. In 1959, from the most famous festival of all, the Bayreuther Festspiel, he sent this report.

A GREAT *TRISTAN* AT BAYREUTH BY WAGNER AND WAGNER

There has been a lot of controversy about the way in which his grandsons are now staging Richard Wagner's operas at Bayreuth, and I had hoped to comment both on *Lohengrin* and *Tristan und Isolde* from this year's performance, thereby covering the early and the late. Unfortunately a combination of delays, and the almost incredible red tape of a garage at Frankfurt (where very nearly as much time is taken filling in forms about the work as in doing it), deprived me of *Lohengrin*.

It may not, therefore, be fair to assess present-day Wagner at Bayreuth on a single performance, but on that one opera, I would say that Wolfgang Wagner's approach is one of sheer genius that makes the work live in its total essence in a way that it cannot ever have done before.

First of all, it may be relevant to say a little about the larger setting. In these days, when an increasing number of Irish car-owners are taking their cars abroad, Bayreuth becomes a practical possibility, especially as it is easy to find very pleasant village-inn accommodation a few miles out and thus save on hotel accommodation.

The Franconian landscape around the town is of rolling uplands, cut into by steep wooded valleys. The red-tiled villages are small details in the expanse of hedgeless patchwork of cultivation, itself given shape by massive clumps of dark forest. There is a Wagnerian quality in the landscape that prepares one for his music.

After all the cult of Wagner-worship, it is surprising to find the pleasant town of Bayreuth seeming almost indifferent to the temple on its outskirts. One would have expected foolproof signs guiding one to it. Instead, it is extremely hard to find. Once found, of course, it is exactly as one has expected, although again there is a marked absence of signs of cult. Perhaps that was only because the season was nearing the end. Or, perhaps, the cult aspect is being deliberately played down as a corrective to the past, especially the immediate pre-war past, when ignoring the whole basis of *The Ring* story, Hitler had tried to identify Wagnerism with his regime.

Whatever the reason, the absence of ballyhoo, of the atmosphere of a shrine of *Grosswagnerismus*, is most pleasant. It is as though the Bayreuth summer festival had settled down to a recognition of the master's greatness as a music dramatist, rather than to be worshipped or trumpeted about.

I had the good fortune to be shown over the stage, thanks to the kindness of Herr Barth, the administrator of the theatre. In spite of electrical machinery and lighting, in spite of closed-circuit television, whereby prompter, electrician, producer, stage manager and others can all see the conductor, in spite of all sorts of modern techniques; the stage is still substantially as Wagner himself designed it, the flies reaching 100 feet above the stage, the machinery extending almost as much below, and the maximum stage depth behind the proscenium being 120 feet. Particularly interesting was the orchestra pit, as designed by Wagner. It stretches *downwards* from the conductor, with the heavy brass at the bottom, and the first violins on the conductor's right. His aim, which succeeds completely, was to weld the orchestra into a single sound, with the firsts as the most important ingredients, and with no sense of individual location or direction of instruments. And the curved reflecting ceilings that achieve this keep the orchestra and its light out of sight of the audience. What a curious contrast to the ideas of stereo recording, with its present emphasis on the location of the instruments.

Though there were some men and a very few women in day clothes, evening dress is really *de rigueur* for the audience. During the long intervals in the falling light, the terraces outside are themselves a lovely sight as the audience strolls to and fro.

Tristan und Isolde has been regarded sometimes as a dramatic failure, as a truly marvellous work of musical art that could equally well make its effect in the concert hall as in the theatre. It is true that there is little opportunity for dramatic action of the recognised sort, no operatic spectacle, little that seems to demand the stage as usually understood. Wolfgang Wagner's new style of production completely changed all that. Throughout the whole four hours it is now impossible not to concentrate and attend through every minute. The type of set he uses has become familiar in photographs. It is a matter of simple geometrical forms first developed in the experimental theatre of Weimar Germany and, especially, by Terence Gray in the twenties at the Festival Theatre, Cambridge. But there is all the difference between asceticism and experimentation of these beginnings and the Wagners' present methods; and no photographs can give any impression of the reality, because photographs are static and clear-cut, while their staging is of its essence soft and changing.

The transition to and from the love-duet of the second act is typical. The curtain parts slowly to reveal a single curved wall covered with dark mauve cloth, a sharply raked stage carpeted (*sic!*) in a neutral shade, a suggestion of trees in the dim background, a luminescent absence of light on the cyclorama. Gradually (and so slowly that one wonders if it is really changing, or whether one's eyes are playing tricks), as Tristan and Isolde take their places down left, they become the centre of five concentric circles of light and shadow, a hazy nimbus of moon develops on the cyclorama and all else is invisible. The whole thing is almost monochrome; the process takes ten or fifteen minutes. The quintessential lovers are isolated from all the rest of the world. They and the audience are utterly absorbed in a beauty not of this world and Wagner's music affects one beyond tears.

So, afterwards, in preparation for King Marke's entry, all gradually changes, great ominous soft-edged beams slope across the sky. The wall becomes an ominous shape.

For all its monochrome, its infinite gradualness, this production is both sumptuous and unobtrusive. It is the perfect realisation of the opera, and one is tempted to attribute to Wolfgang Wagner a genius in its own way equal to his grandfather's. Small wonder that at the very end there was up to half a long minute's hush before ten minutes (by my watch) of tumultuous applause to a black and empty curtain — there are, of course, no curtain calls at Bayreuth.

A curious effect of this production is that it both emphasises a great singer's greatness and minimises another's defects. Thus one could enjoy to the full the stature of Birgit Nilsson's greatness as Isolde. On the other hand, Wolfgang Windgassen was ill on the night I was there, so that Tristan was played by Hans Beirer, a good actor, but a less than ideal singer. In the circumstances, his vocal defects seemed unimportant.

I have not left space to do justice to the real excellence of Grace Hoffman as Brangäne, Franz Andersson's magnificent

Kurwenal, Jerome Hines's majestic King Marke; nor to Wolfgang Sawallisch's completely unified and ideal presentation of the score — though I am bound to say that there were a surprising number of imprecisions and lapses from the orchestra itself.

September 25th, 1959.

SUPERB PERFORMANCE OF *TURANDOT*

The third presentation of the Dublin Grand Opera Society's present season is undoubtedly a winner. Last night's *Turandot* was about the most gorgeous spectacle and most grand of grand opera that the DGOS can ever have presented, in other words that Ireland can ever have seen.

It is impossible to single out any one person or aspect as responsible. That is as it should be. In fact, virtually every collaborator deserves praise for his part in a presentation that really coalesced into something exceptional.

No opera is more spectacular than this. So let us start with Professor Paravicini's scenery, with its typical boldness and brilliance and Ferroni's costumes — not only Turandot's own resplendent ensemble but all of them, and such touches as Calaf's blue contrast to the golds and reds of the Celestial court. With this material and with Harry Morrison's skilful electricining, Bruno Nofri managed a display of colour, shaping, grouping and movement that held me spellbound.

By the very high standards of this production, Act III, Scene I, suffered some confusion and lack of shape, but that is perhaps a hypercritical view of the difficulties of so many characters of what was essentially a drop scene.

Within this framework, Franco Patanè conducted both stage and orchestra so as to give Puccini's striking music the utmost effect — which is saying a lot.

Before coming to the individual principals, I want to praise the National Ballet's dancers. Usually (and inevitably) they seem strangers called in for particular passages. Last night they were permitted to play an integral (and difficult) part throughout, and they were extremely successful. This is also an opera in which the chorus is very prominent. I cannot pretend that their singing was perfect, but it was far better than it has been at times, and both in voice and action they blended well in the total spectacle.

This production is remarkable both for the adequacy and evenness of the cast. Lucilla Udovick is obviously one of the historic Turandots. With a fine voice that commands us across the fullest orchestra, an icy authority and distant beauty that was only in part created by production and dress, she had the rare power to melt suddenly and humanly — to show that Puccini's strange creature was possible and credible.

Too often the Turandot is virtually alone as a singer. It was not so here. Umberto Borsò's Calaf was a real match for her, not only in this odd courtship, but also (one felt) in his future married life. Similarly, Aureliana Bettrami gave Liù a tragedy of devotion, but made her an important character by the dramatic personality of her voice. And Ferruccio Mazzoli's Timur had a true regality from his fine voice and singing.

The three masks (Ernesto Vezzosi, Valiano Natali and Ezio Boschi) fulfilled their half-dignified, half-clownish functions admirably — what a magnificent cloth they sang against! Luigi Bello's announcements were always clear and effective; and Evaristo Orlandini's Emperor was almost ideal (apart from his ridiculously youthful make-up).

If Lucilla Udovick falls very slightly short of my memories of Eva Turner's famous portrayal, the rest seems to me far better than that presentation. Anyone who possibly can should insist on seeing this production now.

27th April, 1960

ISAAC STERN GIVES VIOLIN RECITAL IN THEATRE ROYAL

Chaconne — Vitali
Sonata no. 9 in A, op. 47 — Beethoven
Sonata in D, op. 94 — Prokofiev
Nigun — Bloch
Caprice basque — Sarasate

Considering that yesterday was an ordinary working day for most citizens, Isaac Stern and Alexander Zakin can be well satisfied that there were not more empty seats in the Theatre Royal, Dublin, yesterday. It is extraordinary that, having arranged for Mr Stern to play when most people could not hear him, the Festival should not have put on the recital in the more intimate Gaiety.

Ordinary performers are usually concentrating on giving the best performance they can of the music; they are aware of technical and interpretative problems. Too many of the world celebrities let us know that they know we have come to hear them rather than the music. To Isaac Stern there are surely no technical problems at all, and he is one of those supreme artists whose concern is to bring us and the composer together without any apparent intercession. "Hear," he would say, "what Beethoven has to tell us." He makes music to and with his audience.

Thus he made the old familiar Vitali Chaconne a new experience; rescued *Nigun* from the hands of the too many imperfect violinists and made it a spiritual experience, (how impressive his minimal vibrato was!); and made us share with him the poignancy and the humour of the Prokofiev.

It is probably impossible for a listener to go through twice in 24 hours the previous night's experience with the Beethoven violin concerto. That, rather than the performers, presumably accounts for the "Kreutzer" sonata having a less profound effect on me than I had expected, except for particular moments.

2nd July, 1960

HIGH PRAISE FOR YOUNG CONTRALTO'S PERFORMANCE

Convey me to some peaceful shore — Handel
Spring is coming — Handel
Che farò senza Euridice — Gluck
Frauenliebe und Leben — Schumann
Five Tonadillas — Granados-Periquet
Folksongs — arr. Britten

The Music Association of Ireland held another of their coming-out recitals at the Royal Hibernian Hotel, Dublin, last night. The recitalist was Bernadette Greevy, beautifully supported throughout by Jeannie Reddin.

Before she started the cards seemed stacked against her: a night full of rank smog should be unkind to even an experienced singer, especially if she were to tackle Schumann's *Frauenliebe und Leben* cycle. As it was, Miss Greevy seemed in excellent voice almost throughout — a certain edginess at the end of "Che farò" was surely the weather. And for her to be in excellent voice means a great deal, because she has such a lovely instrument.

It is not the instrument that makes the singer, but the use of it, the artistry, intelligence and musicality. It seemed last night that Bernadette Greevy has all three. She had the presence and artistry to stand simply, giving herself to the audience without tricks of mannerism. She had the sense of meaning to make "Che farò" a piece of opera — we have yet to see if she can act. Her type of contralto voice often goes with complete unintelligibility, but her diction was very clear. Her communication of feeling would almost have convinced us, fog notwithstanding, that "Spring is coming".

On such an occasion to choose the Schumann was either courageous or foolhardy. It turned out to be the former. Perhaps "Süsser Freund" and the last song lacked complete conviction — and no wonder. It needs very great qualities to put across the real emotion with which Schumann invested Chamisso's damp and overheated poetry. But throughout these testing songs Miss Greevy completely held her audience in a way that already famous singers do not always achieve.

It was most skilful programme-building to continue with a group of Spanish songs so unfamiliar that we were at a loss to know what "Tonadillas" are, or whether Periquet is an author or a composer whom Granados arranged. Anyway, they were charming. I suspect that they could have had more insouciance of phrasing, but it was a joy to hear Miss Greevy's agility with the decorations.

These folk-song arrangements of Britten's are among my aversions, but I must admit that they were admirably done.

Altogether this was one of the MAI's best young soloists. May I congratulate her and wish her every success?

19th November, 1960

BERLIOZ WAS A MINOR TRIUMPH AT CROKE PARK

To some people it might seem strange to open an International Festival of Music with a requiem, even one written for a State memorial service on the largest possible scale. Berlioz himself, with his characteristic gift for getting embroiled in difficulties, would surely be slightly less surprised at its performance in Croke Park than any visitors must have been.

For very many of last night's audience, the acoustics of the Hogan stand were no worse than those of the Theatre Royal. Considering how many of the audience were personally there for non-musical reasons, that the open air is unkind to detail, that there were trains, aeroplanes, photographers and birds to distract, the concentration and attention of the audience were remarkable. Two people deserve unbounded praise for this; Berlioz, whose genius created this miracle of music, and Louis Frémaux, the conductor.

Most people in Frémaux's place would have despaired or have run through the event without involvement and with satisfaction if no disaster occurred. Louis Frémaux's very great ability and his entire devotion to the music and his musicians inspired his National Orchestra of Monte Carlo, Our Lady's Choral Society, Alexander Young (standing in for Dermot Troy, who is unfortunately ill) and the audience itself to a memorable occasion. And in view of the differing temperatures and the number of brass instruments all over the place, their intonation was amazingly good.

Later in the week we shall be able to praise the Monte Carlo Orchestra properly. Here let me praise (as well as the conductor) Our Lady's Choral Society. This is far and away the largest amount of singing they have ever tackled. Not only did they know all their music perfectly but they responded to Mr Frémaux's wishes most wonderfully, with numberless small points that make all the difference between the very good and the merely competent. That, of course, can be attributed very largely to their chorus master, Oliver O'Brien.

In last night's peculiar auditorium it was hard to assimilate much of the detail one received. Now that the choir knows the work, it will be a shame if they do not repeat it in the reasonably near future. Could Mr Frémaux be invited to conduct it again, but indoors?

12th June, 1961

A strike by the staffs of all the Dublin commercial theatres was neatly timed for the 1961 Dublin International Festival. For the Berlioz Requiem the festival organisers were able to transfer to Croke Park. Fortunately the weather was perfect, many of the trains were diverted and the presence of Prince Rainier and Princess Grace made it a really gala occasion. **C.A.**
The following night the royal couple attended a student concert at the Royal Irish Academy of Music.

CONCERT IN DUBLIN BY
THE HAMBURG STATE ORCHESTRA

Overture, Oberon — Weber
Symphony no. 4 in B flat, op. 60 — Beethoven
Symphony no. 9 in C, D 944 — Schubert

The Hamburg Philharmonic State Orchestra visited Dublin and played at the Gaiety Theatre last night. While they are treating London to a Stravinsky symphony and one by Fortner, we were given an extremely conservative programme.

In this programme the orchestra showed themselves to be among the best that have visited us. Their strings, especially their first violins, had an enviable gleaming, burnished quality of tone. This does not come from numbers, which are only very slightly larger than our own. Their woodwind had a wonderful refinement of quality — the first oboe's indeed is silky almost to excess. From their horns came such ideal sounds with such perfect control that one wondered how the horn could ever be difficult.

Wolfgang Sawallisch used these forces to give us the essence of both symphonies. Characteristic was the tautly-held suspense of the Beethoven introduction, culminating in a wonderful crescendo on the three notes of bar 35 that really did run from pianissimo to fortissimo, followed by the true violence of the next seven bars and the loveliness of the succeeding softness. This care for Beethoven's intention ran through the whole symphony and created a really felicitous performance.

Almost any performance of the "Great C major" leaves me overwhelmed with the greatness of it. But in few does one get as much satisfaction from its realisation as in last night's. Again, typical instances must suffice — the steady, non-legato, unsentimentality of the horn opening; the sense of radiance as the first subject shone out; the eerie darkening as Mr Sawallisch changed to the second subject in those incredibly short two bars, which in such a performance proved to be quite long enough; the famous trombone entries. Similarly, the almost visible change of colour into the middle section of the slow movement.

And so on through an outstanding performance. Let us hope that Mr Sawallisch will bring his orchestra here again and will trust us with a less hackneyed programme. Now, however, let us be grateful for their playing of Schubert's masterpiece.

4th June, 1962

MOZARTEAN ELEGANCE PLEASES
AT OPENING PROM CONCERT

Symphony no. 41 in C, K. 551 — Mozart
Piano Concerto no. 15 in A, K. 414 — Mozart
Le Sacre du Printemps — Stravinsky

The first of the exciting and extended series of autumn Proms took place at the Gaiety Theatre, Dublin, last night (and is to be repeated tonight in Cork).

Stravinsky's masterpiece and Hephzibah Menuhin's playing of K. 414 had threatened to leave little anticipation over for the "Jupiter" symphony. But also the soft and mild performance of it belied the fact that it is one of *the* great symphonies; and so strong, powerful and majestic that it was nicknamed after the king of gods. And why did Tibor Paul cut his 46 strings to 35 for a symphony composed for over 50? And, while in the complaints department, does the audience have to pay double for eight pages of advertisements in the programme? Is it necessary to plunge us into darkness for the music, and even for the National Anthem and arrival of the conductor?

So much for complaint and now for praise. Hephzibah Menuhin's playing of the concerto was just about perfect — a very strong word indeed. Not only had it all the Mozartean elegance such as will ever be associated with Beecham at his best, but also a virile vigour where needed. This was true Mozart, elegant, stylish, and courtly, but never mild or meek. And as well there was in her playing the humanity and breadth of that universal genius.

If all this was in the spirit of a concerto written for rococo entertainment, her technical means were an obviously personal humanity and a clear scholar's knowledge of style and music. How exquisitely in place every figure was! And, for the matter of that, what perfect proportion and scale to the cadenzas and to the "lead-in" at the return of the andante! These were obviously Mozart's own, and what a lesson to us they are, especially in Miss Menuhin's hands, with a sensitive and loyal accompaniment from Tibor Paul.

And so to *Le Sacre*. It has taken half a century to come from Paris to Ireland, but, of course, was well worth waiting for. There is indeed a sightseer's interest in seeing quite so many wind players on the stage, and gratitude to Tibor Paul for organising it all. But in spite of records, score and history, reality exceeded expectation.

It was so clearly the masterpiece it should be, so absorbing an experience, such spine-tingling music. If you can muster a performance at all, it must be a memorable event. So it was last night. Dare one hope that Tibor Paul and his RÉSO will do it again in the not too distant future?

1st October, 1962

OUTSTANDING RECITAL BY VICTORIA DE LOS ANGELES

The long-expected song recital by Victoria de Los Angeles with Gerald Moore took place last night at the Olympia Theatre, Dublin, and was as lovely an occasion as we had hoped.

Personality is not an irrelevant part of a singer's performance and Victoria de los Angeles has a presence that charms one's heart before she sings a note. Another important quality is diction. She sang to us in Italian, English, French and her native Spanish. Every word was audible in all in an exemplary way, which many singers native to those languages might copy.

The quality of her voice is too well-known to need comment. The quality of her artistry is nearly beyond comment. What exquisite lightness of touch, what delicious delicacy in Alessandro Scarlatti's "La Violette"! What a moving contrast between the two persons in "Death and the Maiden" — which she sang in its original key, such is her range. It was in the other two Schubert songs, "Wohin" and "An die Musik" that she was least successful: the sustained weight of the latter seeming uncongenial. But, by contrast, how apt her Brahms! "Das Mädchen spricht" and "Vergebliches Ständchen" were sung with such understanding and musicality. In "Mainacht" we were given a ravishing treat of perfect tone.

The same artistic mastery, from the inside of the song out, radiated through Fauré's "Les Berceaux", "Clair de lune" and "Chanson d'amour", while I would have gone home happy had I heard nothing but her exquisite performance of Ravel's "Vocalise en forme d'Habanera".

Finally, a Spanish group: Nin's "El amor es como un susio", Catalan Christmas song and "Paño musiciano"; Vives's "El amor y los ojos" and "El retrato de Isabella"; Falla's well-known Seguidilla and Jota and Rodrigo's "De los alamos vengo". In spite of her special authority here, one did not feel any nearer approach to perfection, a comment on her mastery of all the others.

Gerald Moore must have been having an off night. His tone was curiously hard and shallow throughout the dynamic range, and there was less total support and interpretation than I had expected. But, needless to say, even off form Mr Moore is very good indeed.

10th December, 1962

ASHKENAZY RECITAL AT THE OLYMPIA

Sonata no. 9 in D, K. 311 — Mozart
Sonata no. 6, op. 82 — Prokofiev
Twelve Studies, op. 25 — Chopin

Vladimir Ashkenazy, the young Russian pianist who shared the 1962 Tchaikowsky with John Ogdon, gave a recital at the Olympia Theatre, Dublin, on Saturday afternoon. His programme seemed unusually arranged, but it was extremely satisfying, largely because he is such a superb pianist and musician.

As soon as he started playing, one sensed the presence of a master. The start of his Mozart showed that he knew that when Mozart wrote *f* he meant it; and yet his passage work was done with the utmost clarity and that delicacy that only comes from enormous reserves. We could hear, too, in Mr Ashkenazy's playing why Mozart was the supreme pianist of his day, and why he wrote this sonata for his own use at Mannheim.

The first point about Mr Ashkenazy's playing of the Prokofiev sonata was how he made its design and musical shape as clear as if he had been playing Mozart. He showed what all the constituents were and how they fitted together. Next, a part of one's listening could take a physical joy in the necessary and very large technique, using as well great power and (again) the most lovely lyricism and delicacy. This sonata has been described as "violent and despairing." I did not find that on Saturday. Rather did it seem to unite vigour, vehemence, power (an almost Beethovenish power) with tenderness and the many-sidedness of life. Either way, it became in his hands one of the great sonatas of the literature.

When a master such as Vladimir Ashkenazy plays Chopin's second set of Studies complete, receptivity is at full stretch. We not only rejoice in an enormous succession of perfectly and exquisitely presented details of playing and the sensuous and emotional experience of the sound, but can see and hear the united solution by composer and interpreter of the technical and intellectual points of such studies.

Such is Ashkenazy's quality, that, among all the great artists who visit us, his recital surely will remain in our memories as a special piece of musical communication and expression.

11th March, 1963

BRITTEN'S *WAR REQUIEM* AT ST PATRICK'S

It may be that 1963 will be remembered in Dublin's musical history as the year in which Tibor Paul conducted Britten's *War Requiem*. For last night in St Patrick's Cathedral had a historic feel to it. In a few hundred words it is impossible to do full justice to the occasion, so a notice can only skim the surface.

The Requiem was written for a cathedral and obviously benefits from performance in one, even though the particular acoustics of St Patrick's must have added greatly to the difficulties and to those of many of the audience. It is a closely-knit work, in which all the small details are vital parts in the whole fabric and which urgently needs a conductor who can think and feel structurally and also in terms of the whole meaning of it. It would be hard to find an interpreter better qualified to direct it than Tibor Paul. Not only am I immensely grateful for his surmounting the physical difficulties, but far more for such an entirely right and understanding performance.

It was, accordingly, one of the occasions when the RÉSO responded magnificently as main orchestra and chamber orchestra, and any small details out of place were entirely immaterial. The boys of the Cathedral choir sang from the Lady Chapel with clarity, sensitivity, beautiful tone and a surprising immediacy. It may have been a matter of local acoustics but the main choir (the augmented Culwick Choral Society) was weak in volume and in tone quality. It seemed that preoccupation with rhythm and line resulted in the sacrifice of dynamic range in their singing, although the final five bars (and their two previous statements) were beautifully done, revealing the ineffably, sublimely beautiful prayer of the last F major chord.

It was an outstanding privilege to have Heather Harper as soprano soloist. Ideally placed in the pulpit, her utterly true singing, with her perfection of tone and with her unsurpassable artistry and absolute, understanding conviction, made *Lacrimosa* and *Sanctus* marvellous experiences.

Donald Bell was very satisfying as baritone soloist. His invocation "Be slowly lifted up" had the full measure of its scale and his German soldier the right dignity, simplicity and finality beyond hope. And he sang the story of Abram so clearly in conformity with composer's and author's intentions.

David Gallagher's rather hard quality did not seem out of place though I liked his singing least of what I heard last night. But how well he conveyed the hopelessness of "Was it for this the clay grew tall?"

There is no room here to discuss the music itself; whether it is temporary, expressing our times, or permanent and of the company of the B Minor Mass; or the reason for its great effect upon the present listener. That must wait. Let us now thank Tibor Paul and all his performers for the experience, and pray that all the old men with their hands on the trigger may absorb the *Offertorium* into their hearts. Hearing the work, one feels it must be more powerful than hundreds of CND marches.

28th March, 1963

STRAVINSKY CONDUCTS STRAVINSKY

Le Baiser de la fée (1928)
Chorale Variations on Bach's "Von Himmel hoch" (1953)
Symphony of Psalms (1930)

What did it feel like to be in London in 1791 when Papa Haydn paid his famous visit? Surely not unlike being at the Adelphi Cinema in Dublin last night when everyone there rose in spontaneous tribute when Stravinsky walked slowly to the rostrum to conduct his own music. For Stravinsky is as certainly the father of our music now as Haydn was universally recognised to be then.

It also puts a critic in considerable awe. And, as Stravinsky has once more been denouncing critics' ignorance, it is but fair to repeat again that it is the knowledge that it is his job to express his own opinion for the general reader that is the main palliative of the critic's ever-growing awareness of his own ignorance.

Stravinsky's assistant, amanuensis, disciple and protégé, Robert Craft, conducted the complete ballet *Le Baiser de la fée* which occupied the whole of the first half. As those who know Mr Craft's revealing writings on and recordings of modern music are aware, he is an expert on Stravinsky, and a most effective musician. As he conducted the RÉSO last night, it was clear that he is extremely efficient; very, very clear; that he knows what he wants (and presumably what Stravinsky wants), and can get it. But has he any warmth of heart, any real sensuousness? In short, does he *like* music?

For *Le Baiser de la fée* is warm, melodious, passionate music to a considerable extent. It is like a rubble wall whose stones are Tchaikowsky's tunes and whose mortar is Stravinsky. Last night it felt very long; it seemed to need the stage for which it was written; and it lacked sensuousness. If Stravinsky offers it to us as a first half, it must be more continuously exciting than it seemed to me. And the orchestra showed later really spirited playing. So I blame Mr Craft, but also thank him and the composer for the great deal of excitement and flashes of greatness that are in it.

I fail entirely to comprehend Stravinsky's way with words. Apart from *Oedipus* and *In Memoriam Dylan Thomas* he appears to treat them as meaningless sounds. Bach's different treatments of "Von Himmel hoch" are the creation in music of the meaning of the different verses of the hymn. Stravinsky in his arrangement ignores that to the extent of keeping the choir singing the first verse again and again. Why?

Comparisons between this and Webern's transcription of Bach's *Ricercar à 6* are inevitable. The latter is a brilliantly illuminating and wholly convincing commentary on Bach and Webern. By contrast Stravinsky seems to have diminished Bach without putting enough Stravinsky in. Even under the inspiring stimulus of his own conducting, I found myself not enjoying the *music* (not the performance or the occasion) and wondering whether it had in fact been a potboiler.

And so from these two works of, shall we say, indirect inspiration to one of his undoubted masterpieces. I have discussed the *Symphony of Psalms* here at length on another occasion. To hear it alive under its creator was a thrilling experience. Thirty-three years old, it still has a more up-to-date impact than so much more that is far newer.

Here, all the way through, the greatness was tinglingly communicated. And it was communicated through the spirit of the RÉSO, the RÉ Choral Society and the RÉ Singers. Stravinsky's very individual method of conducting — extremely clear, if not always understandable — and the sense of occasion produced an impression that completely overrode several undoubted mistakes. But how much better such inspiration was than mere accuracy. And how grateful to Radio Éireann I am for a historical event not too far away from Mr Handel's appearance in Fishamble Street in 1742!

10th June, 1963

VAN CLIBURN IN SATISFYING CONCERT AT ADELPHI CINEMA

Tone Poem, Don Juan, op. 20 — Strauss
Piano Concerto no. 3 in D minor, op. 30 — Rachmaninoff
Symphony no. 7 in A, op. 92 — Beethoven

The second orchestral concert of Radio Éireann's Music Festival took place last night at the Adelphi Cinema, Dublin, when we had our first opportunity of hearing in the flesh the famous young Texan pianist, Van Cliburn.

The adulation and ballyhoo that surround any pianist of his standing can so easily encourage showmanship and mere bashing; and it was very pleasing indeed to see, and hear, that Mr Cliburn is clearly a sincere and sentient artist of great dignity and restraint.

This restraint in his interpretation may be a little more

than Rachmaninoff himself might have gone in for, but it suited me completely, and is, I feel, more in keeping with our times. Van Cliburn can certainly play loudly when he wants to but with a full and beautiful tone. He seemed concerned at all times that we should hear the music in all its moods and gradations and not just himself. And I found the concerto taking on a more satisfying stature because of his playing.

The Adelphi has the best acoustics for a large concert of this kind of anywhere so far discovered in Dublin, so that a very good balance between orchestra and piano came across and the sound qualities blended very well — but it was a pity the clarinet and piano did not agree on pitch. And the RÉSO played with real warmth to match the music.

Tibor Paul led the orchestra into an impetuous, passionate account of *Don Juan* and after the interval into a characteristically good performance of the Seventh. Was the allegretto a little faster than usual? If so, it was, nevertheless, beautifully articulated and unified. The scherzo had great strength and the finale great fire. With very minor reservations, this concert in a sympathetic hall showed us our orchestra really worthy of itself and Tibor Paul.

17th June, 1963

DUBLIN DEBUT OF CHAMBER ORCHESTRA

Concerto Grosso in G minor, op. 3/2 — Geminiani
Two Pieces for String Orchestra, op. 6 — John Kinsella
Symphony no. 29 in A, K. 201 — Mozart
Concerto Grosso in D minor, op. 3, no. 11 — Vivaldi
Trumpet Concerto — Addison
Sinfonietta, op. 52 — Roussel

One of the outstanding events in Dublin's musical history was the Dublin debut of the Irish Chamber Orchestra in the Examination Hall of TCD on Saturday night. The orchestra was heard last October in Dublin and Wexford in association with the Guinness Choir, and made an extremely favourable impression. It has also played at several provincial centres, and in each case has been highly successful. But only now have we been able to hear it on its own in Dublin. It consists of 17 players (admirably led by David Lillis), most of whom are members of the RÉSO, and it is conducted by János Fürst, already well-known as a violinist in the RÉSO, as recitalist and as teacher.

Owing to problems of tuning it turned out on the night to be impracticable to use the Trinity harpsichord, so that the Geminiani and Vivaldi had to be done without keyboard continuo. The performances were so arresting that they were really enjoyable without it, and, at the same time, so lively that one missed the harpsichord all the more. Another paradox was that the playing of these two was so spirited and full of youthful excitement that they felt stylish; and yet Mr Fürst did not seem aware of the need for decoration. This was a particularly acute problem since there has been on exhibition in Trinity's Library Geminiani's own complicated "Instructions on Gracing a Melody". In the adagio of the Geminiani it became startlingly clear that Mr Lillis's vibrato in the melody was, in terms of Geminiani, but one of the graces of which we should have had plenty more.

The first performance of John Kinsella's serial piece, dedicated to the Irish Chamber Orchestra, was also the first of his music I have heard. The first piece I found very attractive, something articulate expressed by an individual personality.

The Addison of the trumpet concerto turned out to be not John of 1766-1844, but a contemporary American — surely, at a shilling, the programme sheet might have given some information about Addison and Kinsella other than their bare surnames. The music seemed to veer between Copland and Bernstein (is the last movement's resemblance to "I'm so happy" coincidental or deliberate?). The work is slight but a splendid vehicle for a virtuoso trumpeter. Such playing as Thomas Lisenbee's cannot have been heard in Dublin before. It combined the virtuosity of the fairground with the musical sensitivity of a real artist. In his hands the instrument seems as easy as a cornet.

To do justice to Mr Fürst and his players I would like the space of G.B.S. or Ernest Newman. We have had many chamber orchestras here in the last few years. The Virtuosi di Roma are more polished, more impeccable in their specialised perfection. But Mr Fürst has more vitality. The Los Angeles Chamber Orchestra has the vitality of Fürst and nearly the impeccability of the Virtuosi. But Mr Fürst seems to have an ability to display the music so vividly.

This No. 29 has become one of the handful of best known Mozart symphonies. In most performances it is dull — not very long ago Dublin had a performance that was downright bad. János Fürst revealed it anew. His manner of conducting is so expressive and athletic as almost to be a mime translation of the music, but he really does communicate it to his players and to us. The opening allegro was more *moderato* than usual but retained interest all through. He did the repeat and made us feel the musical significance of it as few performers do. The development and recapitulation and coda had more structural point than usual. He showed how the legato and staccato passages had relevance and connection: and how the different melodic phrases were part of a connected musical logic.

The minuet started at a surprisingly fast speed, but it worked, with a beautifully lyrical trio, and again it had point, meaning and life without pomposity. The second movement was truly beautiful; the last with such verve and élan.

If János Fürst and his players can retain this enormous vitality and excitement and their ability to communicate thus the core and soul of the music, there is no reason why they should not be internationally famous. It was not only a joy to be at this concert: it may turn out to have been a historical privilege.

22nd March, 1965

OF STRANGE AND CURIOUS MUSIC

It would need the pen of G.B.S. or the pencil of Gerard Hoffnung to do justice to the remarkable concert (if that is the word) offered to us at the Grafton Cinema, Dublin, at 12.01 yesterday morning — an April Fool's Concert of strange and curious music promoted by Arthur Kalman Presentations in support of the newly-formed Irish Opera Group.

Music is so often pressed into the services of charity that it seems a pity that charity does not support music: or rather that the enthusiastic audience at this concert was not larger since the concert was highly entertaining and put on to help the idea of staging entirely professional Irish productions of opera — something not known yet in our day.

Very properly we started with a highly *Improbable Prelude* by Gerard Victory, a world première played by the Irish Chamber Orchestra (leader David Lillis, conducted by János Fürst) and no less than four well-known pianists at one piano. After that we learnt that with a certain amount of spontaneous (?) additions Mozart's *Musical Joke* (K. 522) can be very funny. Indeed if played by really good players — with a notable cadenza from Mr David (welcome-home-Mr-Dubourg) Lillis.

Not everything was intentionally funny — or rather, intended by its author to be funny. Ebenezer Prout's Duet Concertante for Harmonium (Victor Leeson) and piano (Veronica McSwiney) is ten minutes too long to be funny, in spite of Mr Leeson's high spirited pedalling — tour de France for him next year?

Among the virtuoso performances were Milo O'Shea's abridgment of the Grieg Piano Concerto, his remarkable collaboration with Joe Lynch on two tuning forks in Antony Hopkins's concerto; Joe Lynch's equally remarkable feats on the one-and-tenpenny whistle in Brian Boydell's *Triple Concerto* (Geraldine O'Grady, typist, and Liam Mee, bass vestibule). A remarkable instrument was the Strohviole (a searing, unbelievable, one-stringed instrument) presented by Richard Groocock to the distress of Saint-Saëns's "Swan".

Malcolm Arnold's *Toy Symphony* mustered over a dozen of Ireland's leading singers and players on assorted equipment. This first venture was successful and funny. Many readers will be very sorry to have missed it. I suggest that they send £1 to 31 Molesworth Street and ask Courtney Kenny, the master brain of the venture, for a repeat.

2nd April, 1965

CHEERS FOR EXCELLENT QUARTET

Quartet in E flat, op. 33, no. 2 — Haydn
Quartet no. 1 in C, op. 49 — Shostakovich
Quartet no. 14 in C sharp minor, op. 131 — Beethoven

It is not often that the end of a string quartet recital is applauded with cheering and stamping and if that be thought an incongruous reception to the mystic revelation, the "trembling of the veil", that is the C Sharp Minor quartet it was but the obverse of the deep, rapt participation of the audience in the Aeolian Quartet's performance at the Rupert Guinness Hall on Saturday night.

The performance had just the same qualities that distinguished their performance of the other Beethoven quartets; the same understanding of what Beethoven had written and had meant; the same fidelity to his instructions, in the letter and the spirit. It must be a tremendous physical strain to play this long quartet with such intensity and fidelity. It has no break between all its movements. There is little technical relaxation and no emotional release of tension — the tension changes but does not diminish — right from exploration of the opening fugue to the extreme stress of the last movement. But the players seemed caught up in a performance that conveyed virtually everything Beethoven had to say — and how much that is!

Perhaps the central variation movement was fractionally less penetrating than I had expected. Perhaps only because I used to think this quartet a shade even more wonderful than the A Minor, while as one grows older one comes to experience even more from the A Minor.

Before this climax of the week we had a totally delightful performance of Haydn's "Joke" and one of Shostakovich's first quartet that showed just how close this work is to Haydn's quartets. Both deserve far more space, and both together formed a perfect preparation for the Beethoven.

The cheering on Saturday night was not only heartfelt enthusiastic thanks for the four recitals of the Aeolian Quartet and their choice of programme. It came from a virtually capacity audience who were as deeply receptive and appreciative as any audience anywhere ever, and who were a proof, against the pessimists and philistines, that musically Dublin is no mean city, and one which deserves the Kennedy Hall.

It was also a gesture of appreciation of what Victor Leeson has done for the St. James's Gate Musical Society and for Dublin. He has done something which will be remembered to him for very many years. I hope that last week's audiences and all those who were so strangely and so noticeably absent will enrol rapidly as subscribers to the six interesting looking recitals by Irish artists during next season and to the four recitals by the Dartington Quartet in the third week of next April.

3rd May, 1965

INTERLUDE

WHY DRAG IN THE ANTHEM?
A curious Survival from Victorian Custom

One of the curious customs of the Irish is to play bits of their National Anthem at the end of cinema performances and before concerts. "Curious" because it is not observed in other countries outside the British orbit.

The cinema and theatre custom dates, I understand, from the First World War when it came into force in Britain as a symbolic part of the British war effort..."Confound their politics, frustrate their knavish tricks" as a natural sentiment in times of war. Naturally we took this over with so much of the debris of the empire.

We also took over two associated customs: One is to try to see all the first feature film and yet get out of the cinema before the National Anthem. Even if this is not in order to be at the head of the bus queue or the first out of the car park, it does not in itself indicate any lack of patriotism or adverse criticism of the musical values of the National Anthem. It is just the custom of these islands.

Secondly, there is a tendency on the part of cinema managements to use an aged pre-electric recording, circa 1927, of the Army Band under Herr Sauerzweig. Herr Sauerzweig and his chief, Fritz Brase, did wonders for our bands — and, through their influence, for many fine Irish musicians — but this recording has a certain historic (? pre-historic) quality more interesting to the archivist than to the customer. And, of course in many cinemas it has been played 359 times a year for several years. The result is an interesting sound. Especially when preceding a recital of Liszt's music by one of the world's virtuosi; or after a play with apt incidental music superbly reproduced.

Perhaps it is to deprive us of such remarkable experiences

that Argo have had Our Lady's Choral Society make a very fine recording of the National Anthem on an L.P. disc, where it is given as much dignity as the tune will carry. It is conducted by Colonel J. M. Doyle and recorded with fine modern sound — better, in fact, than most cinemas can reproduce.

So we may now hope that, as long as we retain the British custom of finishing our films with the National Anthem, the actual sound will no longer be a national disgrace.

So much for cinemas. What about concerts? Here we follow the British custom too (of which more in a moment). Usually recitals begin unaided. But orchestral concerts and operas start with the Anthem; and this is a fascinating exercise in reading the musical character of the conductor. Of course it is less so in Cork, where they use Aloys Fleischmann's arrangement (complicated, original and impressive to hear); or at the Curragh, where Captain Mellerick uses what I understand to be his own; or on the visits of the Hallé, where Barbirolli uses another very individual arrangement.

The usual version otherwise is Dr J. F. Larchet's (or a variant of it). This is simple, direct, forthright but able to take the impress of the conductor. Irish conductors tend to have given up the struggle with the tune and just to play it through. Visiting conductors are apt to try hard, as though they did not believe it. Some, like Tibor Paul, make a very real effort to invest the tune with solemnity. Mr Paul indeed went to the length of playing it very slowly and softly, somewhat after the present-day style of playing the German anthem. This was interesting, is known to have pained Dr. Larchet and has not convinced anyone that the tune is capable of solemnity. After all, solemnity was no part of its original life in the War of Independence.

Some stirring and dynamic conductors give warning of their style by injecting *Angst* into the tune and emphasising the trumpet parts. The lyrical tend to phrase it as though it were a Celtic folksong with long singing phrases. Perhaps the best are Italians, who suffer from the only anthem with a less great tune and therefore find ours less difficult to deal with.

And why do we insist on *starting* concerts with our National Anthem anyway? That is another of the many peculiar national customs deriving from Queen Victoria in person. In the fairly early days of the British national anthem it was a prayer for the sovereign and (in peace time at any rate) performances of it were almost confined to personal appearances of the sovereign.

Now Queen Victoria and Prince Albert liked music — Mendelssohn, it may be recalled, described Buckingham Palace as the only really comfortable private house in England, a remarkable indictment. And the Queen decided to honour the Philharmonic Society of London by becoming its patron. Furthermore, she then accorded to it the singular and valuable privilege of being able to regard the Sovereign as present in spirit even when she was not present in body; and therefore of being able to start their concerts with the customary salute to the Sovereign's corporeal presence, *God Save the Queen*.

Gradually of course the reason for the Philharmonic Society's curious behaviour got forgotten and other bodies desiring snobbishly to copy the Philharmonic Society adopted the practice, using their own anthems in imperial lands overseas. As far as continentals in Britain are concerned, it is just one of those odd irrational things the British like doing. As far as *our* practice goes, it is just another of those details that makes it so hard to convince practical people like the Swiss that Ireland *is* different from Britain.

Queen Victoria in stone no longer welcomes our legislators into the Oireachtas. Is it not time she stopped welcoming us in spirit into our concerts?

19th June, 1965

ROSTROPOVICH THE MASTER

Overture, Der Freischütz — Weber
Cello Concerto in B minor, op. 104 — Dvořák
Symphony no. 6 in B minor, op. 74 — Tchaikowsky

Rostropovich at last! After his illness last month, many of us must have been keeping our fingers crossed that all would be well for last night at the Gaiety Theatre, Dublin. It certainly was, and after a curiously Tchaikowskyish reading of the overture here he was, and we waited, enjoying the long exposition, for that glorious moment when the cello starts.

And immediately one felt in the presence of greatness. It is almost impossible for an ordinary person even to find any words to describe his playing, but one must try. Technically his playing is perfection. Just think of all those passages in octaves in the first movement. They were as precisely in tune and blended as when an organist plays an 8' and 4' together.

But only an artist of his calibre so completely submerges the technical in the musical. There was such an effect of total involvement in this superbly passionate and expressive music. He played it so that one heard completely new things in a faithful performance of the familiar music.

Of all the wonders of this performance, nearly the most memorable was his fabulous pianissimo; a whisper, but perfectly clear and perfectly beautiful.

The loveliness of Rostropovich's cantabile and the depth of feeling revealed are beyond words. Perfection is the only adequate idea. Twice in the last ten years have we had a similar musical experience here, the Smetana Quartet's first visit to the RDS and Isaac Stern's Beethoven concerto. Those who had those wonderful experiences will know the effect of this playing.

Tibor Paul did his very best to accompany Rostropovich and the orchestra rose to the occasion — especially the woodwind in the matter of pitch.

I cannot imagine the Tchaikowsky could ever be really suitable afterwards. It certainly was not on this occasion, with every cloying drop of sentimentality squeezed out, including absurd tempo changes to destroy the flow in the second movement and an over-emphasis of the brass that made the third movement seem a vulgar noise. But nothing can tarnish the glory of Rostropovich.

11th July, 1966

R. AND R. SEASON STARTS WELL

The Rathmines and Rathgar Musical Society started their two week's season of Gilbert and Sullivan operas at the Gaiety Theatre last night with a very enjoyable presentation of *The Mikado*. In fact it was one of the best sung and most even of theirs that I recall. And I have only two major grouses. First, that the men's costumes (except for the Mikado and Pooh Bah) were very weak, though the ladies' were good. Second, that Terry O'Connor consistently kept her eyes fixed on her score instead of on her principal singers so that she and they lost each other at every little pull and comma. She directed the ensembles so sympathetically that it was surprising that she would not accompany the solo songs more kindly. Otherwise the spirit and liveliness of her conducting were splendid, especially with such an inadequate number of strings.

This is a fully traditional production, fully in line with the famous prompt book, with Norman Meadmore clearly regarding any idea of *aggiorniamento* as heretical — save (thank goodness) among the Mikado's list of criminals.

Roderick Tierney's well-known and well-loved Mikado was just as before. Joseph Lane's Nanki-Pooh compares favourably with any that I have seen from D'Oyly Carte, while Edmund Barry is a richly traditional Pooh-Bah — in figure, voice, manner and comedy.

It is a pleasure to have such a pretty Yum Yum as Anne Cosgrove and one who can sing as nicely: in both respects she was better than most professionals who have come to us. She was well supported by Catherine O'Connor and Fionnuala Hough as her sisters.

I had not seen Heather Hewson as Katisha before. I expected a treat and got it. Alfred Branagan's Ko-Ko is among the best. He relishes the part in detail. He is beautifully light. He never exaggerates. And it is his own part, not an imitation of anyone else. Added to that he sings engagingly. I found the scene of Ko-Ko's wooing of Katisha particularly impressive. Miss Hewson and Mr Branagan made this a delicious piece of true teamwork. The choral singing was also good.

In terms of the R. and R. and indeed in terms of the professional performances, this presentation is on a high level. And if most of the voices are smaller than those of the D'Oyly Carte Company they were mostly as pleasant, with all the words effortlessly audible. Many thanks, and grand opera singers please copy.

15th November, 1966

WONDERFUL MARLENE DIETRICH

Time is standing still, or rather, has put the clock back, at the Adelphi Cinema, last night and tonight, while one of the great legendary figures of the past recalls that past from "You're the cream in my coffee" and from the intervening days up to Pete Seeger's "Where have all the flowers gone?", and back again to "Falling in love again". Yes, of course, the fabulous Marlene Dietrich. Yes indeed, there is the face and figure that were seen on every screen and every hoarding; that caused tens of thousands of little girls to be christened Marleen. There she is, one would say, unchanged through the years. But surely there is a change? Was she always such a superb artist, such a craftsman? Surely not.

For an hour and a quarter that is long with the amount of material and over too shortly, from her first appearance in that incredible fur confection to her final playing hide-and-seek with the curtain like a kitten, she kept me spellbound, in spite of the very close proximity of a loudspeaker. And of course, amplification is totally right for her for she has always been a screen personality: as well as that, she can really make use of the mike's characteristics — but, while writing this, I have had a call from a customer justly indignant that upstairs there was so much roar from the equipment that Miss Dietrich herself could only be heard when singing in "her marvellous whisper."

Miss Dietrich appears with her own 18-piece orchestra and owes a great deal to the arrangements of Burt Bacharach, but all the way from "Go see what the boys in the back-room will have" and "Boomerang Baby" to the sincere emotions of "Frag' nicht warum" or "White grass neath the stones", it is her perennial artistry and skill! If there are any seats left tonight they are cheap at the price.

29th November, 1966

SUPERB SONATA TEAM AT THE RDS

Sonata no. 3 in A, op. 69 — Beethoven
Sonata in D minor — Debussy
Sonata no. 2 in F, op. 99 — Brahms

It has been quite a time that we have waited to hear Jacqueline du Pré and Stephen Bishop and yesterday at the RDS they proved enormously worth waiting for. And, apart from their individual merits, such a complete sonata team with each partner so clearly right for the other is a rare experience. And after the afternoon recital, it seems strange to recall that they are such a superb team and one hears and takes in the two-fold music as such, and yet one's visual attention tends to Miss du Pré. Perhaps because there are many fine pianists but few cellists on an equal level. And bless them both for none of this piano-lid-shut business: it was very properly on the short stick, so that we had both their full tone qualities.

Jacqueline du Pré is another example of the thesis that great string players have and need great physical strength. I can well imagine her as a swimming champion, where she would use the great strength of her shoulders just as effectively. She attacks her instrument with the same uninhibited zeal that we saw in Rostropovich in the summer. But she is also a flamboyant player using, quite naturally, large and rhetorical gestures. Quite naturally, because they clearly are a by-product of making the music as magnificently as she does. Any lesser player who would imitate them would be both affected and ineffective. In Miss du Pré they are just a part of the conviction of her music making. And what conviction there is too!

There is a passage in the middle section of the slow movement of the Brahms where she played fairly high on the

A string with a most impassioned vehemence while he played with a most profound and lyrical calm. It was a perfect expression of Brahms's writing, but I could not help feeling that hardly another pair would be able to achieve it quite in this way.

In the Beethoven, I found in real life exactly what I wrote about their record in last Friday's record review, and seeing them do it made the reasons so much more right. Again what a pleasure to have such a perfect team where the pianist is the complete equal, in his own right, of the cellist!

I am not sure that Debussy's strange late sonata was not a little extrovert, for all the beauty and balanced reciprocity of the performance.

Such a peak of performance comes one's way comparatively rarely. When it comes from players who have world-class mastery and as well the burning, vehement zeal of youth, the result is something for which one is profoundly thankful.

6th December, 1966

RUBINSTEIN STILL THE MASTER

Sonata no. 15 in B flat, D. 960 — Schubert
Sonata No. 2 in B flat minor, op. 35 — Chopin
Ondine — Debussy
Prelude (from Pour le piano) — Debussy
Forlane (from Le Tombeau de Couperin) — Ravel
Scherzo-valse — Chabrier
The Lover and the Nightingale — Granados
Mephisto Waltz — Liszt

The most remarkable feature about Arthur Rubinstein's

recital at the Adelphi Cinema, Dublin, last night was the large size of the audience considering the almost total absence of timely publicity away from the cinema itself, so that so many regular concertgoers were even unaware that Rubinstein was visiting us. Another surprise was the high cost of the programme — with its remarkable number of misprints. On second thoughts, it was, perhaps, worth half a crown to learn that the second subject of the first movement of Chopin's sonata "leads into a snort."

Of course, the really remarkable feature is Arthur Rubinstein himself. After decades of being one of the world's greatest pianists, he has grown in the last two to being (certainly on disc) the supreme living exponent of Chopin. And now, at 80, he is trotting round the world with apparently undiminished mastery. We are accustomed to 80 being the prime of a conductor's life, but it is astonishing that the stamina and muscular control needed to be not just a great pianist, but *the* great pianist, should be so abundantly there.

I think that Rubinstein's outstanding quality at the Adelphi was his poetry, the poetry with which he shaped a melody, any melody, all through the programme. Especially, perhaps, those of the Schubert sonata, where it is important that the tunes are shown to be the subject matter of the extended work. Rubinstein's poetry made sure of this.

This quality and his exquisite singing touch made the funeral march (and particularly the middle section) so integral a part of the whole Chopin sonata.

It was noticeable that he had chosen the isolated movements and short pieces of the second half of the programme to emphasise colour, melody, touch; as indeed they did, most exquisitely.

It is nearly four years since Rubinstein last visited us. Let it not be so long again.

14th December, 1966

VICTOR BORGE THE VIRTUOSO

Those who have laughed themselves silly watching Victor Borge on television (and who has not?), those who have enjoyed him on the gramophone; they, if they hear him live, as we did at the Adelphi Cinema, Dublin, last night, they will find the experience quite different. For one thing, they will not notice all that deplorable and interfering laughter that stopped them hearing so much — because it will be themselves. In other words, Victor Borge, is enormously better in reality.

Unlike, say, Anna Russell, he does not take the mickey out of the music, but out of himself and of us. And it is a joy to enjoy the utter professional artistry of him. This is of the same order as Marlene Dietrich's — can anyone say more?

At first he almost throws it away. He starts as you might expect, and spins out his routine of not-playing to a point where it is past the beginning of being not-funny. The wisecracks, the Lewis Carroll skill with language, the predictable throwaway jokes begin to wear thin. Is this man really as funny as one had thought? And then, having relaxed you into near boredom, he gets to work, tightening your strings gradually, until by the end of a full programme he has you exactly where he wants you.

Every now and then he invites one to walk on the luscious carpet of deeply sloppy sentimentality, and one wallows or is repelled according to temperament. Then he pulls away the carpet with the perfectly timed joke that leaves one sprawling helplessly with laughter. One never knows, from word to word, what to take seriously and believe (but I *think* it was a serious announcement in the interval and no spoof that brought the exciting news of Louis Armstrong's visit to the Adelphi on July 24th).*

All the way through he is a musician, and expects musical

intelligence from his audience. And he never burlesques anything in a way to deprive us of future pleasure. Even the action accompanying the playing of Chopin's Nocturne as a duet for single-handed pianists will not spoil it, because it remained lovely music as they played it.

They? Yes for he works with Leonid Hambourg as second pianist, a man who fits perfectly into the act and is at least as fine and musical a player as Mr Borge himself. Their exquisite playing of an arrangement of Mendelssohn's *Midsummer Night's Dream* Scherzo was a serious joy.

The three main reasons for the enormous pleasure that he gives are, I think, the finesse of his appreciation of words and language, his fabulous sense of timing, but above all the music in him.

28th June, 1967

* Louis Armstrong did indeed appear on July 24th, 1967.

TIBOR PAUL'S LAST RTÉ CONCERT

Symphony no. 8 in F, op. 93
Symphony no. 9 in D minor, op. 125

Last Night's RTÉSO concert at the St Francis Xavier Hall was the last in a number of ways. The last of the RTÉSO's season before their holidays which they richly deserve (and may they enjoy them!). The last two Beethoven symphonies and the last of this cycle of concerts, and Tibor Paul's last concert as the director of RTÉ's music.

It often happens that a much-awaited climactic event does not quite fulfil expectations. Perhaps the audience expects too much: perhaps the participants' tension passes its zenith. Thus neither of these two symphonies seemed to me quite up to the previous concerts. The Eighth, sunniest of all his symphonies, seemed to foretell a storm: and the right good performance was a little bit anxious.

The Choral Symphony suffered acoustically. The orchestra sounded with less body than usual, which I think was caused by the choir preventing reflection from the back wall of the stage. And its own position at the back of the stage behind a low proscenium arch, and with the soloists at its front row meant that all the singing was as from a distance. Once again, if only we had the Kennedy Hall.

As far as I could hear all the soloists (Irene Sandford, Bernadette Greevy, Edwin Fitzgibbon and Harold Gray) were in very good form. And in detail Mr Paul was giving us a worthy performance. But for me, I shall regard his "Eroica" and his Seventh as the high spots of this month.

Tibor Paul's final series of concerts has been turned into such a display of sensational emotionalism, apparently by the group of people whom musical Dublin has been calling the Fan Club, and by a number of others who are rarely seen at musical events otherwise, that some summing up of Mr Paul's work as conductor seems not only desirable but necessary in addition to comment on last night's final concert.

A fairly strong body of opinion (especially among those who rarely if ever listened to the RÉSO before Mr Paul's day) are convinced that he has vastly improved its quality. Memory, of course, is an unreliable guide, but I have the strong impression that if the tape of Mr Paul's first performance here of the Seventh (on November 14th, 1958) be compared with that of last week not all that much difference will be shown: and I very much doubt if the tape of the "New World" under Silvestri on June 30th, 1960, would prove in any way inferior to Mr Paul's most recent performance of it.

On the other hand I think it is true that Mr Paul has more often enabled the RTÉSO to realise the potentialities which it had before his arrival than other conductors have done. He is certainly a past-master of the great occasion, and, in good form undisturbed by over-anxiety, emotional stress or overwork, he can give performances such as we have heard this month of music from Beethoven onwards. A romantic at heart, he can take us to the very core of Bruckner, Mahler, Brahms and Tchaikowsky. His sympathy with and understanding of Richard Strauss is almost uncanny. But he can also display the necessary self-discipline to produce very great readings of Beethoven and, as his Eurovision *Messiah* in April proved, he can learn to communicate the music of Handel of whose period, up to then, he had shown himself to have very little understanding.

The one really good action, musically speaking, of the first Director-General, Edward Roth, was to appoint Tibor Paul as principal conductor of the RTÉSO. Unfortunately, Roth followed it with what has seemed to me a disaster for us and for Mr Paul himself, his appointment as music director responsible for all RTÉ's music programmes of every kind for the last five years.

This is not the place to comment on Tibor Paul as music director, because we are here concerned with him solely as conductor. But I believe that the strain (and the actual time involved) in carrying out two men's work caused even him to rely too much on his recollection of the scores he knew intimately, to be unable to expand his repertoire as much as he would have done otherwise (especially of modern music), and also to let the emotional strains of overwork interfere with his personal relationship with his orchestra. Thus, too often in the last five years, his performances were below what he had himself trained us to expect from him, especially when the power of the music slipped into dynamic violence, or emotion into sentimentality.

I am convinced that, if Tibor Paul had refused the second job, he would have been able to lean on the support of a director, would have been far more often at the peak of his musical power and would be remaining with us with the honour and respect of the orchestra, the Authority, and all the public.

While the apparent ineptitude with which RTÉ handled their dealings with Mr Paul last autumn would be incredible were it not characteristic, it is a matter of very great regret that he did not accept the surely valuable invitation to remain principal conductor without all the other responsibilities (had he really any desire to direct jazz and folk and pop?). This last series of concerts has been exciting witness to what I have so often written of here, his ability to secure really great performances from our orchestra. Most sincerely I hope that in the future he will often return as guest conductor, that RTÉ will have the wit to invite him and he the stature to accept. No matter whom we may have here in the future, there will be particular performances of Tibor Paul's that will always be highlights of our musical history. Meanwhile, let us wish him not only the right engagements, but that he may be able to fulfil them always at his best.

29th July, 1967

At a Wexford Festival reception in Guinness's brewery, Dublin. From left: Charles Acton; Dr Tom Walsh, founder of the festival; and Sir Alfred Beit, Bart., chairman. In the background is W.B. Porter, public relations officer of Guinness. 1988. (Photograph: Lensmen)

INTERVAL

CORRESPONDENCE

THE BOSTON CONCERT

Sir. — Your music critic, C.A., in his letter of August 29th has been kind enough to invite my opinion of the playing of the string section of the Boston Symphony Orchestra; did they play with "feeling, depth and love"? With all diffidence and with profound obeisance to the experts, I can lay my hand on my heart and say (so far as I was able to judge in a building so vast that much of the vitality was sucked out of the tone) that the playing by this massive body of strings was all that could be desired and approached the regions of genius.

I am at a loss, however, when the subject of an orchestra's soul is brought up. I find myself wishing that the critic had used his space to give us a proper account of what musically had taken place. When a really great orchestra and its conductor are denigrated I feel cheated if I am not told exactly what it is that I have overlooked; in fact, I feel that your urbane and kindly C.A. is doing less than justice to all if, in support of such condemnation, he gives us merely some talk about boring playing. Your critic, by the way, is now so certain about the playing being boring that it is only fair to those who organised the visit of this illustrious body of musicians to say that your critic's view is not necessarily shared by musicians and certainly was not shared by the audience. [...]

4th September, 1956

**

In a Cruiskeen Lawn article (20th January, 1960) Myles na Gopaleen "wondered whether all this pother for a concert hall in Dublin is genuine at all or whether it is another item in our limitless repertoire of humbug" and felt that "there are far too many halls in Dublin, many of which could be easily converted for the purpose of music recitals."

CONCERT PITCH

Sir, — Please accept my expression of regret about Myles na Gopaleen's illnesses and my best wishes for his recovery (January 20th).

His observations about existing locations show signs of persistent aural defect or of that most serious disease, chronic absence of body from concerts.

His misquotation of my article of January 14th reveals a very distressing illness, *caecitas lectoris*, the inability to read the words upon which one comments. The prognosis is not very hopeful.

The concert hall (which we do need) is far more than a single auditorium. Apart from its other contents, it must include a small hall for 350-400 people, *as well as* halls for 700-800 and for 1,500 people. But for his *caecitas lectoris*, I think he would have found my meaning plain. Perhaps, sir, you could devise a suitable course of treatment for so valuable a citizen.

Charles Acton, 21st January, 1960

***

The leader in *The Irish Times* of November 10, 1962 pleaded (alas in vain) that the design that won the prize sponsored by the E.S.B. for the premises in Lower Fitzwilliam Street would not be realised in concrete.

REBUILDING DUBLIN

Sir, — Notwithstanding your admirable leader on Saturday, perhaps I may appeal for support from architects and others in another most desirable project, that of replacing the scherzo in Beethoven's Fifth Symphony by a more useful movement. After all, this existing scherzo is over 150 years old and therefore past its best; everyone is by now fed up with its reiterated da-da-da-dum rhythm, the joke of the double-bass start to the trio (if it ever was a joke) has worn very thin. And we would have the chance of a fine independent movement in which we could get rid of that untidy link into the last movement, with its boring drum solo (150 repetitions of the same note proving Beethoven's lack of inspiration). A nice new movement in well-mannered good taste should surely not detract from the view of the whole symphony.

One anxiety will remain. How shall we succeed in destroying all the scores and parts of the existing movement in case there are tiresome people who prefer it? We would-be musical vandals are at a disadvantage compared with the E.S.B. who will have been able, once for all, to "murder a beautiful building" (to quote Sir Basil Spence, architect of the new Coventry Cathedral) so that "the world is the poorer, for that particular light has been put out for ever."

Charles Acton, 13th November, 1962

***

DIFFERENT STANDARD

Sir. — The reviews of your music correspondent, Charles Acton, are certainly controversial, thereby presumably selling papers and making him a successful journalist. Nevertheless, I would dare to ask a question which Mr Acton dared to ask of Josè Iturbi last week: "Is he also a musician?"

In his review of last Saturday's RDS concert he described Valerie Tryon's playing as "tidy" but having "no fire, no passion, little vitality", etc., etc. Her partner in this concert, Alfredo Campoli, the world famous violinist, described her playing to me as "fabulous"...this comment was unsolicited.

Visiting celebrities are sensitive to criticism. Last Saturday's paying audience was generous in its applause. Mr Acton's standards must differ.

26th March, 1968

***

RTÉSO CONCERT

Sir. — I have read Mr Acton's unnecessarily worded criticism of the playing of some of the members of the orchestra in last Sunday's night's symphony concert at the Gaiety. I would ask one simple question: "Could he play these passages himself?" I would add that the concert-goers and musicians of Dublin would have more respect for the music critics of this city if they could be assured that these critics had musical expertise and professional experience of orchestral playing to back up their criticisms and the "musical authority" to entitle them to express their opinions.

14th October, 1969

RTÉSO CONCERT

Sir, — Miss L. in her letter published in your paper on October 14th complains of Mr Acton's criticism of the playing of some members of the RTÉ orchestra at a recent concert, and asks, "Can he play these passages himself?", implying that no-one should criticise unless he is an experienced performer himself.

This is nonsense. What particular instrument would Miss L. require Mr Acton to play — violin, viola, cello: what instrument from the brass or woodwind section, the tuba perhaps, or the percussion instruments, or them all?

Musical criticism is something far above personal performance. The ability to judge and compare and comment comes from a long study and a deep knowledge of music past and present.

Anyone who makes a practice of reading what Mr Acton writes on the subject of music, either about live performances or in his most reasoned and erudite articles about gramophone records, must realise how well equipped he is for his job.

17th October, 1969

***

WEAK VINEGAR

Sir, — I must take exception to the fact that your music critic, Mr Charles Acton, compares my cousin, C.V. Stanford, to "weak vinegar" in relation to two spirituals and "The last words of David" by the contemporary American composer, Randall Thompson.* It is a pity that Mr Acton will not be considered eminent enough as a composer to be buried in the Musicians' Corner in Westminster Abbey, as my cousin is, or to have a memorial service in his centenary year as my cousin had, and at which Dr Vaughan Williams was present. He (Dr Vaughan Williams) was one of my cousin's many distinguished pupils.

23rd June, 1970

* Acton actually wrote that Thompson's piece seemed like "Stanford and weak vinegar".

WEAK VINEGAR

Sir, — May I congratulate Miss S. of Waterford on contributing (June 23rd) what must be one of the most hilarious letters ever printed in your frequently quite hilarious correspondence columns?

I am sure that your Music Critic must be severely troubled — nay, confounded — by the realisation that, after all, he may not now enjoy the everlasting benefits of interment in Westminster Abbey.

25th June, 1970

* * *

RTÉ CONCERT

Sir, — Charles Acton makes heavy weather of a misprint in an RTÉ concert programme (March 3rd). Perhaps it is cavilling, but I counted eight errors — misprints, misspellings and mistakes of grammar — in Mr Acton's review.

10th March, 1980

RTÉ CONCERT

Sir, — I can only thank Mr R. for his letter; and apologise to him (March 3rd). He counted "eight errors — misprints, misspellings and mistakes of grammar" — in my notice.

I myself counted 18 misprints, no misspellings and only two mistakes of grammar (both misprints of punctuations).

On the other hand, a daily newspaper has only a few hours between material being written and being out on the streets, while Mr R.'s organisation had weeks if not months to print its programme. In fact, on the title page of the programme booklet in question, there were no less than 33 errors, not counting the title of Mozart's penultimate opera which RTÉ called *Die Zaburflote* which I tried unavailingly to reproduce. [...]

Charles Acton, 13th March, 1980

SONG TITLES

Sir, — Your music critic, Charles Acton (July 7th) very rightly deplores printing blunders of song titles. The worst I know of happened many years ago when Plunket Greene, the great bass, was asked to sing at a concert in Co. Tipperary. He sent in three songs (1) "The Kerry Cow"; (2) "The Erl King"; and (3) "The King in Thule." This is what the audience read in their programmes: (1) The Heavy Cow"; (2) "The Eel Ring"; (3) "The King in Thurles."

10th July, 1970

* * *

DÚN LAOGHAIRE ARTS WEEK

Sir, — As an outsider who visited and thoroughly enjoyed the Dún Laoghaire Arts Week, I consider that your critic Charles Acton was extremely petty-minded, inaccurate and unfair in his report.

We are well used to critics, especially Mr Acton, indulging in hair-splitting and applying professional criteria to amateur performances and events, but it is difficult to accept these, especially when the better qualities, and indeed any good points, are ignored in an effort to demolish yet another amateur cultural effort.

Even if we can ignore his lengthy and largely irrelevant comparisons with other widely differing events, it is difficult to understand why your critic should concentrate on petty deficiencies and make inaccurate statements about the nature of the arts week.

While making his petty criticisms about opening hours, free admission and the like, he studiously avoids any evaluation of the excellent material presented, and gives no encouragement to organisers, exhibitors or performers. He mentions people who could become involved and ignores those who are! There is no mention of exhibits in the wide-ranging art exhibition, of the sculpture, copper-work, paintings and mixed-media presentations! Mr Acton thinks it sufficient to question closing times and the audience to whom the week is directed. [...]

The efforts of the artists and organisers are worthy of more than Mr Acton's attempt to belittle them. I enjoyed them as did the full houses throughout the week. Long may the arts week flourish!

18th September, 1975

* * *

Sir, — Surely Mr Acton should confine himself to musical criticism in his reviews and not resort to making personal insulting remarks about the artists? In his recent review of a concert given by the Dublin Orchestral Players he said that the orchestra was gradually being reduced to "an ill-organised elderly women's club" due to the fact that the majority of its members were female and over 50 years. Is 50 too old for a musician? Does Mr Acton think that Tortelier, Menuhin and Rostropovich and other such internationally famous artists who have reached the grand old age of 50 should retire? And why is he prejudiced against women?

The quality of the orchestral playing and the interpretation of the works is all that should concern the music critic. If this recent programme of the DOP was poor and of a low standard, by all means let Mr Acton say so, but age and sex have nothing to do with the matter. I wonder how many of the RTÉSO are over 50? What about ageing music critics? When should they retire?

6th June, 1977

* * *

COUGHING IN CONCERT

Sir, — [...] I have come to certain conclusions about audiences' coughing, conclusions assisted by the late Séamus Kelly, who had a very long experience in the spoken theatre as well as in the lyric theatre and concert hall. There are several sorts of cough in concert, but two sorts are especially noticeable [...]

First, obviously, is the genuinely unpreventable one, with various physiological causes, which afflicts all of us from time to time, and which we do our best to suppress, whether with lozenges, with stuffing handkerchiefs in our mouths, or, extremely, leaving the auditorium. One can have nothing but sympathy and commiseration with sufferers from it.

There is also what I have described as the inconsequential cough. [...] Long experience taught Séamus Kelly and me that these coughers had not the courtesy to reduce the impact of their coughs upon their neighbours [...] Observationally, what I have called "inconsequential" coughing does seem to vary with audiences' absorption, interest or boredom.

Charles Acton, 4th April, 1984

* * *

AN ECHO OF CICERO

Sir. — Mr T. asks you if I could give some reasons for my dislike of the term "senior citizen".

1. I dislike hypocritical euphemisms, especially when they become meaningless. If, as superstition, the ancient Greeks preferred to call the Fates the "Eumenides", fair enough. We are all entitled to our superstitions. But to invent, as some American do, this term "senior citizen" (hereinafter "SC") was not only coining a euphemism for an old age pensioner (hereinafter "OAP"), but a condescending one with its implication that there is neither dignity nor pleasure in old age and that old age must be concealed or glossed over.

2. If Mr T. wants to call himself "old citizen" in Latin (*civis senex*), let him, but the language does not alter the fact and I prefer to call myself old in English.

3. Like most OAPs, I am a contributory old age pensioner, but when I call each week at the post office I do not want anyone condescendingly to suggest: "O dear, we must not say that the poor old bugger has come to collect his OAP — he

mightn't like it — let us say that he has come to collect his SC's entitlement and he won't mind."

4. There are occasions in daily, social life when the tactful euphemism oils the wheels of social intercourse. But when a euphemism like this becomes a regular term, it becomes meaningless.

5. SC now means OAP and that is that. And doubtless California will soon produce a new euphemism for SC, as it has become debased, as is the fate of nearly all euphemisms — consider the constant search for new words to describe the places of human defecation and certain sometimes terminal diseases.

Most pensions are the result of actuarial contributions, and therefore of entitlement, implying no dependence or charity. The Head of our State draws three pensions as well as his salary (as do some others of our legislature). Do we regard him (or them) as "dependent" or "in receipt of charity"? Mr T. himself receives a pro-consular pension through the British Imperial Government. I am sure that he does not regard that as charity, any more than I do.

6. "SC" is usually used in terms of reduced admission price. Getty and Howard Hughes were undoubtedly senior, and presumably citizens of the USA. Were they candidates for cheap tickets?

Finally, Sir, I have seen a new gobbledegook word arise, "the unwaged". Never mind that Getty may also have been unwaged, to be unemployed through no fault of one's own is a real deprivation and a euphemism may extremely well be in order, but that is very different from Mr T. refusing to be called, in plain English, "old", as I am happy to be.

Charles Acton, 5th June, 1985

Charles Acton at home. April 1989. (Picture by Colm Henry)

*Acton interviewing Sir Andrzej Panufnik at Carrickmines in 1977.
(Picture by Camilla Jessel, the composer's wife)*

TRIUMPHANT END TO BRAHMS RECITALS

Six Piano Pieces, op. 118
Variations and Fugue on a Theme by Handel, op. 24
Scherzo in B flat minor, op. 4
16 Waltzes, op. 39
Four Piano Pieces, op. 119

Julius Katchen brought his great series of four recitals of the complete piano music of Brahms to a magnificent conclusion last night at the RDS. And as one now draws breath, one would like to lean back and take stock.

First, however, this final evening, with a programme of mostly well-known works of great appeal. For all the change in Brahms from beginning to end, even in the penultimate pieces, there can still be found the turbulent flood of notes with which his earliest works can dazzle us. As Mr Katchen played the Scherzo (the earliest surviving work of the composer), one wondered that two hands and one piano could encompass so much. And yet with such virtuoso music, Mr Katchen has always a melodic line and a thoughtful, intelligent message: if only pianists who can get round this sort of music would use it instead of the insignificant displays they so often produce.

Some time ago, a German pianist at the Institute played these Handel variations in a quasi-Handelian baroque spirit. It was most interesting as showing how deep was Brahms's intuition of the depths of Handel's theme. This memory made all the more satisfying Mr Katchen's totally right and authoritative view, not of Brahms through Handel's spectacles, but of Handel through Brahms's and also of the gradual complete overlaying of the Handel air by Brahms's thought.

I wish there were space to discuss the other items in

detail. Let me confirm Mr Katchen's view of op. 119 as emerging from gloom into radiant light. And it was a very great joy to hear that final E flat Rhapsody driving on in triumph, with flexibility but without the excessive pulls and gaps that almost all other pianists give us.

However, this last recital should be seen as part of this great series. Let us salute the bravery of the promoter, Michael Emmerson, in offering it to us, and express a very deep gratitude. I suppose if he were to ask Julius Katchen to do it again in a year's time, too many of this year's audience would not return. But I feel that we have been initiated into a great experience; an experience that (especially in the two middle recitals) will have a greater effect in the future when our spirits have digested it. And that I shall properly experience these performances only next time I hear the music; whether from Mr Katchen himself or from anyone else.

13th October, 1967

MUSICAL PERFECTION AT THE RDS

3 Slow Preludes with Transcriptions
  of Fugues, K. 404a — Mozart and Bach
Trio No. 2 in G, op. 9, no. 1 — Beethoven
Divertimento in E flat, K. 563 — Mozart

When people upbraid a critic for not going overboard about something which is only very good, they forget that he, because he attends more events, knows that the very good is far from perfect, and that he must keep his full supply of superlatives available for perfection. And yet when perfection comes his way, the critic feels even more powerless than usual to do justice to it in mere words. Having emerged from the RDS yesterday afternoon, feeling to be purring and grinning like a Cheshire cat, the problem was how on earth to do justice to the Trio Italiano D'Archi.

Here was the quintessential perfection of string chamber music playing, the sort of thing that only comes one's way every couple of years or so with a visit from them or from the Smetana Quartet. Indeed, my memory of the Italian String Trio was so glowing that I went straight to the RDS in some trepidation, in case I had exaggerated their excellence and might be slightly disappointed. I need not have worried, for this recital was completely of the same standard as its predecessors.

Most chamber music groups are made up of people who are, in fact, not soloists, partly because soloists tend to go for the larger rewards of solo playing, partly because usually the personality required for solo playing is almost the antithesis of that required for the true democracy and co-operation of chamber music playing.

In this case Franco Gulli (violin), Bruno Giuranna (viola) and Giacinto Caramia (cello) are real soloists, with soloists' standards of tone and performance, and yet they work in perfect harmony as a group. Individually, not only are they soloists, but they have, each of them, a most beautifully creamy quality of tone, and real depth in their tone and interpretative phrasing. As well as that, as well as their innate understanding of what music and chamber music are about, they also have that uniquely Italian quality of gaiety, of enjoying life and work, of treasuring cantabile and of caring about every least, most insignificant-seeming note. Every rapid auxiliary note matters, as does every mere harmonic repeated quaver. Other groups may strive for and have these qualities of musicality: but other groups have not got the magnificent technique as well.

These three slow Mozart preludes with their following transcribed Bach fugues are not only rarely heard, but they are also a sizeable, serious chunk of music with which to open a recital. But the Italian String Trio rightly judge that their audience wants to be taken thoroughly seriously. We know how seriously Mozart responded to van Swieten's introduction to him of Bach's instrumental music. If we did not know, we could hear it in these intense and deeply thought preludes.

Beethoven's string trios are full of difficulties, not merely the usual ones of rhythm and phrasing and interpretation, but particularly his penchant for writing for violin and viola in octaves, or for all three instruments in octaves. It was a wonderful experience to hear the Trio playing this work effortlessly in the full spirit of Beethoven, with the sense of fullness as a quartet; and with each part distinct and enjoyable at the same time as partaking of a complete ensemble. All these qualities were, of course, fully evident in the Mozart trio which somehow became even more of a great masterpiece than our normal experience, and yet at the same time (especially in the variations and the finale) became the sheerest possible, most happy delight. It seems all too long since this Trio last visited us. The more often they come, the more I will be pleased.

20th February, 1968

PIANO MUSIC WITH A DIFFERENCE

Aloys Kontarsky's recital of all the piano music of Karlheinz Stockhausen in the Hibernian Hotel, Dublin, last night certainly turned out to be the momentous occasion we had expected. And, before all else, I would pay tribute to Mr Kontarsky himself. Here was technique and sheer virtuosity of a high order, the dedication one expected and an obvious utter authority.

Musical specialisms of all sorts have their devoted advocates; but it is seldom that these are such first-rate musicians in every way. And, in addition, Mr Kontarsky put us much further in his debt with an introductory talk about the pieces, which was not only extremely helpful, but also expressed with great charm in beautiful English.

Not the least element was the reaction of the audience, which had an encouraging number of young people, and which also included a gratifying number of regulars. The 24 minutes of No. VI were listened to with an absorption, an attention and an absence of coughing that were much greater than at very many average concerts of ordinary music. One could write a long paragraph of conclusions about that alone.

The difficulty about this music is that there is so little for an inexperienced audience to catch hold of. As Shawe-Taylor has pointed out, ordinary music depends on melodic or harmonic expectations being fulfilled or interestingly cheated. With Stockhausen there are not expectations, because we are not able to grasp the principles of organisation. It was, in fact, one of the striking lessons of the recital that all through the evening it was obvious that this was all the product of a very high degree of organisation with nothing whatever haphazard about it, even if one had no clue about the reason for the details one was hearing.

The works consist of 11 "piano pieces" (*Klavierstücke*). After the opening No. VI, with its 24 minutes of complexity, Mr, Kontarsky played No. IV, which group themselves like the four movements of a standard sonata (lasting about seven minutes in all). Perhaps because more concentrated, perhaps because without the points of silence or repose between groups of organisation, these seemed to me more difficult than VI. On the other hand, No. IX with its hundreds of repeated chords, and its more orthodox elements of specific chords, seemed much nearer normal experience and indeed to be exciting and interesting.

One could hear in the "suite" of V, VII and VIII the concentration of particular problems: and in the aleatory XI, where the player may choose the order of the elements and their tempi, it seemed that Mr Kontarsky made an element of pattern accessible to the listener. Even more so in No. X, which used more strange techniques than the others, including all sorts of clusters from soft murmurs to veritable assaults on the keyboard with the whole forearm, strange and fascinating glissandi, all sorts of effects of pedalling or of resonating strings, there were, at times, emotional kinships with Chopin and Debussy, and at others dramatic new experiences.

It is remarkable how much was accessible at this first experience. If the German Institute were to bring Mr Kontarsky back again to play the same programme, would he have the same size of audience? And would we get a much deeper experience? I, for one, would very much like to know.

29th February, 1968

COMING-OUT RECITAL BY JOHN O'CONOR

Sonata No. 11 in A, K. 331 — Mozart
Sonata No. 23 in F minor, op. 57 — Beethoven
Scherzo No. 2 in B Flat minor, op. 31 — Chopin
Images (first series) — Debussy
Sonata No. 3, op. 28 — Prokofiev

Accompanists cannot have coming-out recitals as such; and John O'Conor has shown himself to be an accompanist of real ability. Similarly with repetiteurs, musical live-wires, teachers, and so on; and John O'Conor has already been making a name for himself in all these fields while still a student.

In the previous solo piano appearances of his that I have heard, technical prowess was a long way behind musical intention.

Accordingly, I confess that I approached his coming-out recital at the Hibernian Hotel, Dublin, last night with the reflection that Gerald Moore was universally condemned by his teachers in his student days as one who would certainly not make the grade, but also with some anxiety, since a coming-out piano recital must mean that the player is now ready to compete on level terms with every established soloist already in the business.

It is therefore with very great pleasure indeed that I most warmly congratulate Mr O'Conor on an extremely successful recital that opened my eyes to his merits as a piano recitalist. His very programme was either chosen with audacity or calculated courage — almost certainly the latter — since it included a Mozart sonata that nearly all his audience had played, the "Appassionata" about which everyone has strong feelings, and this Chopin scherzo.

In fact his performances were very satisfying. I could argue about many details of the Mozart, but it was a mature, convincing performance. For all that, I do not understand why he omitted the repeats of the second part of all the variations (and similarly in the minuet), thus making his birds fly with one and a half wings. Fortunately, he did not carry this error into the Beethoven and he was entirely right to omit the large repeat in its finale.

The major impression of his Beethoven was maturity and

power; and therefore a feeling for the total structure and the beautiful, warm, singing quality of tone that only power can get, whether loud or soft.

It was fascinating how far more enjoyable this performance was in every way than had been that of the renowned American pianist* the previous night.

And there were all sorts of details that contributed to this enjoyment, such as John O'Conor's ability (rare enough) to give his rests their proper value, never to anticipate Beethoven's crescendos, to give the exactly contextual stress to *sforzandos*. But there were all sorts of other details which brought a warm nod of approval as the performance developed.

These qualities of understanding and realisation informed all the rest of the programme, each item in its own way. Certainly the whole affair was a great pleasure, and on this showing anyone who engages Mr O'Conor should be sure of getting real musical satisfaction.

13th November, 1968

* Charles Rosen

SVIATOSLAV RICHTER AT THE RDS

French Suite no. 2 in C minor, BWV 813 — Bach
15 Variations and Fugue in E flat, op. 35 — Beethoven
Pictures at an Exhibition — Mussorgsky

There are a certain few supreme artists whose performances are among the experiences of one's life, more or less no matter what they do. Such a one is Sviatoslav Richter, who played at the RDS on Saturday night (presented by David Laing) and who was to play at the Belfast Festival last night the same two works but with Schumann's *Etudes symphoniques* instead of the Mussorgsky. This has been Mr Richter's first visit to Ireland.

There is immediate certainty with him that one is hearing a really great master. There is no question (as so often happens) that this famous man has been over-rated: that never arose. His approach to the Bach was one of simplicity. Clearly he was aware of the qualities of the harpsichord — notably the remarkable plucked quality of his left hand, neither *staccato*, not *legato* nor even *détaché*, so much as conveying jacks rather than hammers. But, equally, a direct, simple, almost unsophisticated right hand whose penetrating thought was revealed in its clarity and distinctness. With all of that went the curious fact that the first five movements were totally unadorned, even the traditional mordents being omitted, while every practical note in the gigue was decorated.

An interesting detail was that Mr Richter added a second minuet. Is there any evidence for its inclusion?

These Beethoven variations (nicknamed "Prometheus" since he used the theme earlier in *The Creatures of Prometheus* and also "Eroica" since he again used it later for the finale of the third symphony) are musically very slight. Was it not a waste to have the master spend a third of his precious time on triviality? All right, given the two outside works, why not something that would not have produced excessive weight but that would have been more worthy such as one of the sets of Chopin studies?

On the other hand, I felt that we experienced, almost, Beethoven's reasons for writing them and something of what his performance must have seemed like. There was, of course, never any question of pretending that these variations had the profundity of the Diabelli ones, for example. Nonetheless, it was fascinating to see and hear Mr Richter enjoying the muscular, musical, rhythmic experience of them. They were no matter of showy Lisztian floridness, though they did display their performer (as doubtless their composer) revelling in displaying muscular prowess and patterning by musical means. There certainly was an element of "Look Mummie, no hands!" but what superb pleasure it was just to listen to and watch the doing.

I would like to draw attention to so many details of the Mussorgsky, such as the cursory haste of the initial "Promenade" before the visitor's interest was aroused, and the commenting effect of its later appearances; or the inexorability of "Bydlo" for all that Richter starts loud and not soft as marked; the clacking of the women's voices in "Limoges"; the fabulous excess of the "Great Gate of Kiev"; as Mr Richter made them all so much clearer than anyone else. But there is just not room.

The ordinary performers, good and bad, can be praised and blamed, analysed and accounted for: but there is a special class of the really great ones. Whether they are right or wrong in any detail, by any ordinary standards, is irrelevant. Just to have heard them is the true experience. The experience is the message. We have now experienced Sviatoslav Richter.

18th November, 1968

DOWLAND CONSORT'S FAREWELL

Come again, sweet Love; Weep you no more sad Fountains —
Dowland
Sweet Honey-sucking Bees — Wilbye

Tanzen und Springen — Hassler
O Musika — Peuerl
Thule, the Period of Cosmography; Come Sirrah, Jack, Ho! —
                                                    Weelkes

The silver Swan — Gibbons
On the Plains, fairy Trains — Weelkes
Scendi del paradiso — Marenzio
El grillo — Josquin
O dolce mia vita — Nola
L'amanza mia si chiama — Azzaiolo
Contrappunto bestiale — Banchieri
O primavera; Lasciatemi morire; Quel augeltin che canta; Si ch'io vorrei morire — Monteverdi
Ave Maria — Josquin
Sanctus, Benedictus and Agnus Dei from Five-part Mass: Justoram animae — Byrd
Lo tacero; Invan dunque; Moro lasso — Gesualdo
Mon cœur se recommende à vous — Lassus
Au joly joly bois — Jannequin
Petite Camusette — Josquin
Petite nymfe folastre — Regnard
La nuit froide — Lassus
Mignorine, allons voir si la rose — Mauduit
Draw on sweet Night — Wilbye

Exceptionally I have written out the full programme which the Dowland Consort sang in the Examination Hall of Trinity College, Dublin, on Saturday night; partly because I think readers will be at least interested in that as in any other thing about the event; and partly because it is likely to be of future historical interest just what such a group, and this group in particular, most wanted to sing out of their repertoire of over 300 works.

After all, they have been singing for 11 years; they quickly achieved a very high standard indeed, being ready within a year to two to accept the supreme challenge in the Renaissance field, of Monteverdi and Gesualdo; and to take their place as equals of the Sestetto Luca Marenzio, then the world's leaders in the business. If such a group of ten artists, after such a career, choose this particular 10%, that is both an insight into their tastes and standards, and the most valuable critical approval of these works. No one knows as well as the frequent professional performer any work, or its powers of enduring satisfaction.

I have just referred to their level footing with the Sestetto Luca Marenzio. Thanks to the difference between Italy and Ireland, the sextet were whole-time singers whose tours abroad were sponsored by the Italian government; so that while we first heard them here at the Italian Institute, their achievement and renown induced the RDS to engage them in the ordinary professional way. Not only did they directly participate in creating the present international image of Italy, but groups such as the Dowland sprang up after them. For none of the Dowland Consort is full-time singing possible. Therefore their touring abroad has been very strictly limited and as well, the international lustre they could have shed on their country has been denied by the absence of Government sponsorship.

Without doubt the frustration of these facts has contributed to their decision to disband. As they started Saturday's farewell concert, the intense musicality of their phrasing, the exquisitely graded softness in their opening madrigal made the conservationist in me rail against the destruction of such artistry, the removal from Irish life of one of its international standard achievements. However, if they do not desire to continue with enthusiasm, they are better to break up now than risk the decline that would accompany half-heartedness.

I have praised their work and style so often already that it would be tedious to do so again. Suffice it that after their two hours' programme, ending with the best singing of the evening in "Draw on sweet Night", they told their large audience that they were prepared to go on singing all night as long as anyone wanted to stay. I myself left after their fourth encore, since the beauty of their performance (and the music itself) of "Innsbruck, muss ich dich lassen" was so moving that it was impossible not to feel in it the *Nunc Dimittis* of the later "O Welt..." version.

On this occasion one must name them: sopranos, Eilís O'Sullivan, Cáit Lanigan, Gráinne Yeats, Mary Boydell; contraltos, Enid Chaloner, Hazel Morris; tenors, Richard Cooper, George Bannister; basses, Tomás Ó Suilleabháin, Brian Boydell (director). Over the years they have made audiences all over Ireland their friends: so many of them were in TCD to give final thanks. It was a privilege to be among them.

10th November, 1969

JANET BAKER'S SUPERB REGAL ARTISTRY

O had I Jubal's Lyre — Handel
Sleep, Adam, Sleep; Sweeter than Roses, Alleluia — Purcell
Frauenliebe und Leben, op. 42 — Schumann
An die Musik, D. 547; Die abgeblühte Linde, D. 514; Die Männer sind méchant, D. 866; Epistel, D. 749 — Schubert
No. 1: Chanson d'amour — Fauré
Mandoline — Debussy
Serenade — Gounod

It surprised me that the RDS member's hall was not packed out on Saturday night for the recital by Janet Baker, accompanied by Martin Isepp. I doubt if all the other potential listeners were in the other part of the RDS.* But wherever they were, they missed hearing one of the truly great artists, and one, surely, at the height of her powers.

One can sense the advent of a great singer on the approach to the platform, and it only takes the first phrase to prove it. So it was on Saturday. Miss Baker had in her voice, her singing, her communication the same regal quality that had informed that superb Dido which I was privileged to hear in Scottish Opera's *The Trojans* two years ago. This was a similarly moving experience to that.

In this recital she did us the honour of including a number of unusual items with the better known ones. Thus the familiar Handel, triumphantly sung, went with three far less usual Purcell items, all sung with a craftsmanly enjoyment of executing Purcell's florid rhythms.

Janet Baker has such control and finished artistry that she can relax the muscles she does not need to use. If her interpretation calls for dropping her hands at her sides, then they are visibly relaxed. Contrariwise, if she tenses, it is deliberately to convey tenseness. So, too, she has brought her art to the point where she acts each song with all her voice, face, body and mind as though it were her total, real, present preoccupation. So in the Schumann, from the eyes-downcast private thoughts of "Seit ich ihn gesehen habe" through the open exaltation of "Er, der herrlichste von allen" to the numb emptiness of the last song, she acted the songs as though she were the girl yet without allowing one to realise, as it was happening, that this was a totally professional performance — or that such artistry cannot be achieved unless it is totally professional and controlled. And in this cycle, as throughout, Mr Isepp's accompaniment was just right.

In the Schubert group, after melting one's heart with the sheer beauty of "An die Musik", she could give us "Die Männer sind méchant" (a humorously indignant and dramatic obverse of "I know my love"), and the operatic parody "Epistel", so that we could enjoy the humour, the parody, the joking, and at the same time the inherent music of both of them and her singing on all the various planes. Considering her brilliant word-painting, her ability to put over the individual words and their sense as a whole (not to mention her perfect diction), the programme, at 10p, might have given us literal translations of the words. This would surely have helped.

I have run out of space before coming to the French group. Never mind: one must run out of superlatives about what surely has been the recital of the year, if not of the decade.

22nd February, 1971

* At the Fianna Fáil *Ard-Fheis*

INTERLUDE

A MUSIC CRITIC'S THOUGHTS ON THE SONG CONTEST
(Excerpts)

[..] People who were most vociferous against the Eurovision Song Contest and our participation in it and who were most surprised that I, a serious music critic, approve of it and enjoy it, take their dim view because they think it is culturally bad. They regard it as trivial, or as being bad pop, or so much less than we should be doing. Of course it's trivial; of course the tunes are of no particular merit. The only surprising thing about these songs is how widely they seem to stay in people's memories — unlike the ordinary pop song, which seems to die much more quickly. But is it bad pop? It certainly isn't ordinary pop, or ordinary song.

The competition has by now arrived at a "song for Europe" style. Even among the national winners in each year there are a whole lot of songs which are quite clearly not trying to be songs in their own right but which are trying to get so close to some previous winner (for example *Puppet on a String*) that they may pull it off by sheer imitation. The panel to choose the eight songs for the national contest, of which I had the privilege of being chairman this year, was much impressed by the number which were obvious attempts to be a "song for Europe" rather than a song. But an indifferent song for Europe is no worse than an indifferent pop song of any sort.

Perhaps the difference between us serious music critics and other writers is that we regard virtually all pop songs as hopelessly trivial and in themselves totally unimportant. Literature has its Westerns; its slushy romantic novels, its comics: music has its pop of various sorts. Were broadcasting to find a literary equivalent of the Eurovision Song Contest — say to find a new comic strip, or the best mottoes for Christmas crackers — the writers of Westerns and romantic novels might dash contemptuously into print, but the good poets, playwrights or critics would probably be far more tolerant.

So, if one is going to have pop music — and one is going to have it — let's have an entertaining show like this which does at least have people attending and which, let's face it, has in the last seven years done an enormous amount to show the ordinary continental that Ireland is not (a) Holland, (b) Iceland or (c) part of the west of England. [...]

As I say, if you are going to have pop, I see no reason why you shouldn't settle down and enjoy having an international party like this one. It is far far preferable to have it once than to have the continual day-in, day-out brainwashing of background pop, of daily trivia with pop, of pop-magazine programmes, of pop everything that, to my mind, does debase the standards of a community. Getting blind drunk once a year is far less injurious than being only just sober every day of the year. [...]

8th April, 1971

SHOSTAKOVICH ATTENDS DUBLIN CONCERT

The Four Seasons, op. 8, nos 1-4 — Vivaldi
Serenade for Tenor, Horn and Strings, op. 31 — Britten
Chamber Symphony in C minor, op. 110 — Shostakovich

The English Language Institute are once again doing Dublin proud by presenting three concerts in July by the New Irish Chamber Orchestra in St Patrick's Cathedral, the first of which took place last night (the next will be this night week).

A very great extra interest was added by the presence of the great Russian composer, Dmitri Shostakovich, at the whole concert, culminating in the performance of the Chamber Symphony in C minor which is in fact an arrangement of his eighth quartet for string orchestra by Rudolf Barshai, conductor of the Moscow Chamber Orchestra. So successful an arrangement is it that one easily forgets its origins and hears it as though it were conceived for the medium. Furthermore the NICO and André Prieur, their conductor, gave it an absorbed and wholly convincing performance. The presence among us of one of the greatest of living composers lifted the whole concert onto a different plane.

It seemed fitting that that work should be preceded by a work by Mr Shostakovich's friend (and dedicatee of the 14th symphony) Benjamin Britten. Frank Patterson was the tenor and Victor Malirsh the horn. The latter encompassed the difficult part beautifully, the gradations of his soft tone and sensitivity of phrasing fitting especially the acoustic of the building. To my surprise the building did not support Mr Patterson's voice as I had expected it would, but he sang the cycle most expressively, catching the changes of colour completely, especially between Blake's "O Rose thou art sick" and the "Lyke wake Dirge" and in the cantilena of the final Keats sonnet.

I feel it would be helpful to applaud between concertos in the Vivaldi. A dozen movements divided into distinct works need more break than courteous and expectant silence from the listener's point of view. And, though Mary Gallagher gave no such impression, it must be hard on the soloist too. This was a delightful performance all through. As she is the NICO leader, the rapport between her and the rest was naturally complete, and in the context the balance between them was singularly happy. She had, to my surprise, a touch of insecurity in the last movement of summer, but for the rest she and they gave a performance which combined elegantly the purely musical pleasures of the works and their descriptive pictoralism.

6th July, 1972

CONCERT OF EARLY MUSIC IN TCD

The St. Sepulchre's Consort gave an accomplished concert of medieval and renaissance music on Friday in TCD

The Consort are now four who are primarily singers (Vanessa Sweeney, Lucienne Purcell, Peter Sweeney and John Milne, in order S.A.T.B.) and five instrumentalists, Barra Boydell (who appears to be the leader of the group), Jennifer Robinson, David Milne, Andrew Robinson and Honor Carmody. They play recorders, crumhorns, shawms, a rebec, viols, tabors and a bodhrán. Mr Boydell and Mr Robinson divided between them the very clear introductions to the music.

This group is always welcome as one which treats its work seriously and achieves a strictly professional standard. They have now adopted a uniform of a simple brown top garment, looking like a medieval smock, and they manage their platform movements with a deft precision. All of this is extremely welcome and fits in with their nearly impeccable recorder playing, their very good work on the other wind instruments and their fully achieved ensemble.

They took us from an Italian 14th-century saltarello, via 15th century Burgundy, 15th and early 16th-century France to the England of King Henry VIII, and finally the early Jacobean. A genre that I found particularly interesting and entertaining was the combination of two songs together (e.g. "L'homme armé" and "Il est de bonne heure né") where it helped greatly to have each song in an independent setting first.

I understand that some medievalists elsewhere are turning their backs on the strident, quasi-Arab or more or less sean nós, vocal quality, to which Margaret Wilson introduced us here. But this style was maintained on Friday by Miss Purcell and I was delighted to hear Mr Sweeney achieve it in tenor terms (and what an excellent entertainer he is!). My own ignorant view is that this quality is probably right for the medieval music (and Mrs. Sweeney should strengthen hers and Mr Milne attempt it) because, like chivalry, bellied instruments and so much else, the spring of much of the secular music of the time was Arab. But also, I think that Miss Purcell should use a more modern, western quality in later work.

Thanks to this Consort, we are now really having our musical horizons pushed back pleasurably. As they progress, they can only learn more and more and if they continue to pass it on with such a high standard, we can only be the gainers.

5th December, 1972

A GREAT *ELIJAH*

As I write (on Thursday night) I have just come from the RDS at the end of the most wonderful performance of Mendelssohn's *Elijah* that I have ever heard. And I have heard a number, having grown up in the days when no season was complete without its couple of *Elijahs* to match the three or four *Messiahs*.

Unlike the latter, which can surmount the grisliest performances, *Elijah* faded away under the discouragement of the bad and the sloppy. But one has only to hear it well done to be moved by its musical and dramatic strengths and recognise it to be a great work.

When it comes to a tremendous performance like that of Victor Leeson and his Guinness Choir (a happy issue to them out of all their afflictions!) not only can it be thoroughly cathartic, but it is something else. If Sam Thompson's "The Evangelist" displayed the weaknesses of our brethren in the north-east, to know and to hear the first half of *Elijah* ideally performed is to be shown or to be reminded of their strength and their faith and their soul — as perhaps *Gerontius* or the Verdi *Requiem* might symbolise our other brethren. We need to be shown.

Victor Leeson had taken his usual meticulous care in preparation. The choir sang magnificently throughout, and they are as much the essence of the work as Elijah himself. For the angels of "Lift thine Eyes", Ethna Barror's Lindsay Singers sang from the gallery at the back, and that even they were not better than the main choir shows the latter's accomplishment.

For the single and double quartets we had Mabel McGrath, Cáit Cooper, June Croker, Maura Frewen, Frank Dunne, Richard Cooper, Peter McBrien and Joseph Dalton making excellent ensembles, with the four ladies particularly good in the magical *Sanctus*.

Raimund Herincx was a magnificent Elijah. It is a great dramatic role as well as one with some glorious music. Mr Herincx was as moving in the despair before the Lord's coming as in the opening curse, or his tremendous invocation of God's fire.

Irene Sandford was exactly what I want the soprano to sound like here. Her "Hear ye, Israel" was exquisite. Bernadette Greevy allowed both what dramatic strength she has in the Jezebel music and the splendour of her singing at its most heavenly in the angel's music. The impression of faith and simplicity in "O Rest in the Lord" surely put her singing of it among the greatest of the work's 120-odd years. Only David Johnston, the tenor, was less pleasing vocally, but not enough to detract from the whole. The clarity, assurance and fine intonation enabled treble, Clive Carr, as the messenger boy to take his place beside Mr Herincx.

I was sad that too often some members of NICO occasionally did not respond to Mr Leeson's conducting, but, again, that was only a ripple on the surface of a wonderful experience.

1st June, 1974

OPERA PREMIÈRE IN CHRIST CHURCH

If Monteverdi's music and his perfect marriage of music and emotion can move you to tears, if you can agree with me that no composer ever has written more divinely beautiful music, then go to Christ Church Cathedral where the Dublin première of his first opera, the marvellous *Orfeo* is being presented as part of the Theatre Festival.

The question has been asked whether "opera" should be part of the Theatre Festival. If one asks about the state of the theatre in a great many countries in Europe, people will assume that "theatre" is just as much lyrical as spoken. Opera as much as "straight." Yet we learnt that this festival had allocated over £5000 to "Crock" (enough said) and £300 to *Orfeo*.

This vast discrepancy is reflected in certain qualities in Christ Church Cathedral. Not that one need worry about scenery. Admittedly in Mantua in 1607 a lot of money was spent on gorgeous scenery; Apollo, the *deus ex machina* descended in his chariot from on high: and so on. But the Victorian elaboration of Christ Church's choir screen can make one imagine a Venetian Byzantine magnificence and, as anyone with any theatre experience knows, it is for the producer and the work to make the audience see what is not there. To a considerable extent Anne Makower and her forces succeed in doing so.

Allowing for the fact that Monteverdi's contemporaries were trying to recreate the classical Greek theatre, the "pastoral classical" costumes of Lona Moran and Robert Lane's masks are consistent, even if I felt that the dark and light stone of the cathedral should have been complemented by more magnificence of colour. And there is about too many of the singers (solo and chorus) an atmosphere of earnest amateur work rather than triumphant professionalism.

And I felt that Eric Sweeney, conductor and editor, had been a little too willing to put up with the practical rather than demand the utmost possible. For instance, it is reasonably established that Monteverdi scored Thrace for recorders and such like, and Hades for sombre trombones, crumhorns and a regal.

That contrast was an inherent part of the theatre. So, too, Orpheus's persuasion of Charon included many different sorts of music reinforcing him — violins, then trumpets, then recorders and so on. For all the splendour of Theresa Costello's violin playing, Mr Sweeney should have summoned more sonorities to speak for Orpheus.

In spite of that, and some well-meaning but not totally polished performances among the singers, there is so much that is good, so much that allows Monteverdi's own fabulous creation to move us, that the whole presentation is a triumph.

There are two glories, two triumphs of the performance. One is Mr Sweeney's devoted servitude to the music. The other is Frank Dunne's quite wonderful performance of Orpheus himself. We are already familiar with him as a very fine singer, but to get so much inside the style and individuality of Monteverdi is something far more. I found myself moved to tears by his "Possente spirto" — and I went there with a fair knowledge of it. In any other country such a performance might bring fame.

Within his shadow, there were a number of very good performances — by Paul Deegan as the shepherd beautifully stylish and theatrically felt, Pádraig O'Rourke as Charon and Pluto, Edith Forrest as Proserpina, Shirley Blood-Smyth as Hope and Music, Thomas Wilson as Apollo.

10th October, 1974

INSPIRING CONDUCTOR WITH RTÉSO

Symphony no. 83 in G minor — Haydn
Violin Concerto in D, op. 35 — Tchaikowsky
Pictures at an Exhibition — Mussorgsky-Ravel

At the last concert but one of the season at the St. Francis Xavier Hall last night, Charles Dutoit conducted our RTÉSO for the first time, and with really inspiring effect.

Tall, slim, with gestures that are elegantly expressive and very French, he gives the impression of the acting ability of Marcel Marceau, the showmanship of Leonard Bernstein, the total involvement in the music of Cleo Laine. A conductor's demeanour has no necessary relevance to the performance he gets from his orchestra, but in some cases his visible personality is a description of what he evokes. Certainly I felt last night that, had I been watching him without sound, I would have imagined the effects I was hearing.

He made of the Haydn a symphony substantial enough to have made its great effect in Paris, without exaggerating its scale. Everything was tautly in scale, each phrase exactly thought and balanced. I would guess that Mr Dutoit is a perfectionist who, if given enough rehearsal time, would produce performances of a Toscaninian meticulousness and excitement. We got very close to that last night in a stuffy hall and at a time of year when the orchestra are usually showing signs of end-of-season tiredness.

The Mussorgsky was a triumph. Far too many people take the *allegro giusto* of the opening "Promenade" too fast. Mr Dutoit took it *giusto*, as one would walk if getting a general view of the exhibition before looking at individual paintings; and took each later promenade as directed and not (as too often) at the same pace. He made Ravel's fabulous orchestration as colourful as it should be, evoking brilliant and beautiful playing from everyone, and made the paintings vivid before one's eyes and the music marvellous in one's ears. At the time it felt the best performance of it that I had ever heard.

Brian McNamara's performance in the concerto was surely the most impressive that he has ever given here. He took the first movement at a very deliberate speed. It could be that he was taking no chances in a formidable piece. It could also be that he feels it like that, as though virtuosos down the decades had gradually whipped it up for effect. Certainly it made the first subject even more Tchaikowsky and Russian than usual: I liked the air and the expressiveness he gave to all the melodic line; and I found that the bravura passages had musical merit and not virtuosity.

One result was that the first movement was definitely long, but he and Mr Dutoit made it a most impressive one. Perhaps there were small signs of lack of assurance early on, but by the cadenza these disappeared and thereafter he had authority and, in the slow movement, the sweetness and moving cantabile that used to inform his playing when he displayed his very first promise.

19th July, 1975

TURANGALÎLA A GREAT TRIUMPH

Over the years the memory collects a very few peak occasions — Otto Mazerath's Bach Mass, Barbirolli's last *Gerontius*, Stern's Beethoven concerto, the first Dublin visit of the Smetana Quartet, Stravinsky at the Adelphi, Rinaldi's first Violetta with the DGOS are some. Saturday night's performance by the RTÉSO of Messiaen's symphony at the St Francis Xavier Hall is the latest.

In spite of the anticipatory excitement of hearing this famous, strange and somewhat rare work, expectation was tinged with anxiety. Rumours emerged from rehearsal that it was unbearably noisy, that it was an hour and a quarter of uninterrupted boredom, that it was repetitious and monotonous. That the performance ended with an unprecedented amount of cheering from the packed audience showed that more than me were bowled over by the experience.

The score does not demand more forces than, say, Strauss's "Heldenleben" or "Zarathustra", let alone Schoenberg's "Pelléas" — but it sounds as if it did. It must be strange for individual players, but both the quality of sound and all the details confirmed the feeling in the hall that our orchestra were rising magnificently to the occasion and it was also clear that Albert Rosen was excelling even himself in a devoted, faithful and completely true performance.

It had been indeed a pleasure to learn privately on Friday night from one French diplomat that Messiaen himself was much impressed by and full of praise for Mr Rosen, and from the Ambassador himself that the composer had commented to him with great enthusiasm about our splendid orchestra. To us, of course, neither is any news, but in a nation of knockers it lifted up the heart to hear of a notoriously *exigeant* composer expressing himself privately thus. And I hope that the fine artists of the RTÉSO will feel encouraged by this exterior praise.

On special platforms in front of the apron were the piano soloist Yvonne Loriod, and the Ondes Martenot soloist Jeanne Loriod — incidentally in matching dresses (one red, one orange), adding brilliance to the scene, which I am told were by Chardin which accounts for their splendour. I have nothing to add to my already expressed vast admiration for Yvonne.

None of us can be connoisseurs of the Ondes, but I am in no doubt Jeanne is the instrument's master. As for the instrument itself, it looks very impressive. Being very nearly the first electronic instrument, it probably takes up a lot more space than such an instrument would if devised now. And I presume from the score that it is capable of much wider varieties of tone colour than Messiaen used here. In the empty hall, apparently, it had seemed disproportionately loud. In the full one, its balance was perfect. As used in this piece on Saturday, it had sounded like a real musical instrument, and I was not conscious of any loudspeaker sound quality. Presumably it was largely Miss Loriod's own artistry that made it seem a human and musical instrument unlike most electronic things. And, certainly, in her hands the effect of it in unison with the full string choir was deeply beautiful and emotional.

A number of impressions of the work itself remains. An emotional continuity through its ten movements that makes it an overwhelming unity. An immense and unexpected variety of timbre — if one may whisper a comment about his piano and organ music, both of them have restricted palettes — *Turangalîla* included all the varied brilliances of a Lurçat and a Jack Yeats; with constantly changing colours and great contrasts between movements. Perhaps it was dominated at times by tremendous gong sounds, but they but emphasised this continuing variety.

Again, it was full of strangely immediate tunes; less banal than Mahler's, less repeated than, say, Beethoven's in the finale of the "Pastoral Symphony". It was a sensuous, sensual, physical, emotional wallow; but what, pray, is wrong with that? I do not know how much one would enjoy it if one heard it as often as Beethoven VII. But that is unlikely to happen. I am quite sure that it has to be heard in live performance for one to receive even a tenth of its impact. I am equally certain that on Saturday night I had one of the major musical experiences of my life.

12th January, 1976

DO-IT-YOURSELF *MESSIAH* IN MONKSTOWN

For the first time in Ireland (as far as is known here) *Messiah* was performed with the audience as the choir last night. Monkstown Parish Church was packed with nearly 1,200 people (a couple of hundred more than anyone thought it would hold) for what has become known affectionately in advance as the "Do-it-yourself" *Messiah*.

To be precise, the main body of the church was filled with this choir, divided into the four voices while the three galleries, the space below the west gallery and the chancel were full of the non-singers. Leading the choir and among them were the members of the Third Day Chorale from Bayside whose musical director, Marie O'Shea, conducted the proceedings — after a charming introduction (including various necessary instructions) from Gay Byrne.

There was an orchestra of ten strings consisting primarily of the Testore Quartet and their friends splendidly led by Colin Staveley — his work was all the more important since Miss O'Shea as yet lacks instrumental conducting experience. And, while she knows exactly what she wants and can get it from the choir, she is not yet aware of the necessity of a keyboard continuo throughout the work — arias such as "Rejoice greatly" sound very odd with nothing between the top line and the bass of the orchestra and solos accompanied only by two cellos make a nonsense of Handel's intention. In future she should have a harpsichord in the orchestra or have the organist play the continuo.

The organist was Douglas Williams, who did not have the knack of anticipation when he was playing, and who therefore was not always with the strings. It was, however, a very great pleasure to hear these very fine string players in such dedicated stylishness.

Neither Mary Sheridan nor June Croker were at their best,

the latter in particular dragging portentously behind any speed she gave Miss O'Shea. Richard Cooper, on the whole, was singing very pleasingly; and William Young was magnificent as usual.

As I had to leave after the "Hallelujah Chorus", I was deprived of hearing Szabolc Vedres's trumpet obbligato.

The making of this enormously enjoyable performance was, of course, the mass choir and Marie O'Shea's assured and inspiring direction of it. She took good lively speeds, got really splendid ensemble and the precision and vitality of all the choruses and was inspiring to hear and watch. Obviously this is going to be an annual event.

23rd December, 1976

CZECH PHILHARMONIC AT RDS

Vltava — Smetana
Piano Concerto no. 3 in C minor — Beethoven
Symphony no. 8 in G, op. 88 — Dvořák

We are all further in the debt of the Royal Dublin Society for presenting last night in its Main Hall a concert by the Czech Philharmonic Orchestra, the first visit of a great orchestra of international standing since the demolition of the Theatre Royal — not that that was acoustically practical as a concert auditorium. And it is interesting to note that it took 4,250 people at prices of £5 down to £1 to more or less balance costs and receipts, in spite of the premises being virtually rent free.

In every way, this was a great and memorable occasion and all I want is more space to put down my impressions.

Before enthusing about this great and wonderful orchestra, I must praise the RDS and its hall.

It was a bitterly cold night, but the hall was warm. Over 4,250 people require a lot of care to seat and get their cars parked, especially more or less on a pilot run. Betty Searson and her helpers had it all so organised that the concert started nearly on time with no sense of stress.

Last year for their *Messiah*, Our Lady's Choral Society performed in the middle of one long side of the Main Hall and the sound was dull and muffled, presumably because it lodged in a bay of the roof. Last night the orchestra platform had been built at the far end. As a result, the sound in the centre nave was lovely.

I took the first two works in the excellent seats I was given and had the loveliest experience of orchestral sound since the Phoenix Hall (which only held 198). For the symphony I went to the very back, too far away to see their detail, but the sound was still warm, clear, full and lovely — far better than in the Kennedy Center in Washington or Lincoln Center in New York (where I have heard comparable orchestras). I was told that it was poor in the side aisles — where another time the cheaper seats should be.

For great occasions, like last night, the Main Hall is really good for orchestral purposes. The question now remains: how many of the 4,250 (or of the 400 or more who couldn't get tickets) will come back on another occasion without the curiosity of a first time? Even more interesting, how many of those 4,250 regularly (or ever) listen to their own RTÉSO, whom they should be proud to hear?

Admittedly, the RTÉSO are not the Czech Philharmonic and the RTÉSO has a maximum of about 75 musicians, while the visitors numbered about 120.

There is no doubt that the CPO deserves its fame. Czech string players have a uniquely beautiful sound anyway. In their orchestra they are breathtaking, quite apart from their fabulous authority and richness in their own Smetana and Dvořák.

The quality of last night's Czech string playing was infinitely moving even when they are only holding accompanying minims in the concerto. They thereby beautify the playing of the soloist.

And it should be a matter of pride to us that in John O'Conor we have a pianist who can rank with them. This was a large-scale but very sensitive performance. In a concerto that often seems to play itself, Mr O'Conor showed how a fine performer can bring out the inwardness of Beethoven's thought. the splendour of the first movement, the stillness of beauty in the second — all with complete partnership from the orchestra thanks to the mediation of the conductor, Zdenek Kosler.

Partly because of the hall, partly because of the orchestra, but mostly I presume because of the conductor, the equality, the matching style and intensity of strings, brass and woodwind was a thrilling experience. In the symphony, one could be stirred by the full brass choir or by a penetrating solo trumpet, but neither ever drowned the other choirs and all had their own beauty. But I could go on for twice as long about the details of this magnificent performance.

30th November, 1977

MUSIC THEATRE FROM FIRES OF LONDON

Prelude and Fugue in C sharp, Bk. 1 — Bach-Davies
Stedman Doubles — Davies
Chamber Symphony, Op. 9 — Schoenberg-Webern
Miss Donnithorne's Maggot — Davies

Last night's instalment from the Dublin Festival of 20th Century Music was at the RDS and was the climax of the visit of Peter Maxwell Davies and his The Fires of London, and, whatever we may have made of their work, this visit has been one of the most important contributions to our experience that the festival had made in its decade of life. And I am deeply grateful to the British Council and the British Ambassador for these remarkable experiences.

On Tuesday night Mr Davies's own work was a short part of an extraordinarily mind-stretching evening. Last night he was the protagonist. His instrumentation of the familiar Bach was as revealing as Webern's of the Ricercar half a century ago — and it is to Webern that we must look for a parallel rather than to, say, Elgar or Henry Wood, on the one hand, or Swingle or Loussier on the other. The marimba may seem odd for Bach, but the sum total is a bewildered desire to hear it again to see if the result was really an "X-ray analysis of the motivic element". Judgment reserved.

The movements which we had from *Stedman Doubles* were a fascinating tour de force of composition for clarinet and oriental hand drums, and of performance by David Campbell and Gregory Knowles. The latter's work was breathtaking to see and hear: and the former gave us what I think must have been our first Bartolozzi tones here.

After that Webern's compression of Schoenberg's 15 instruments into five seemed almost ordinary, although played with virtuosity and musicality.

If I had not heard Mr Davies's enthralling lecture about Music Theatre and Miss Donnithorne on Monday at the John Player Theatre, I think that I would have been nonplussed. Thanks to it I found the work and its performance (with Mary Thomas in the title role) absorbing.

The text is important and we were provided with it. The music is so written that I doubt if anyone could hear more than some salient verbal tones in performance. The staging uses lighting. Bearing in mind that the house lights were always on for the first two and a half centuries of opera, I think this should have been taken with half house lights rather than none.

Miss Thomas and her colleagues (with the composer conducting) gave a magnificent and disturbing performance of a very strange work which I am still mulling over and trying to assess for myself. All I can say now is that I am immensely grateful for the chance to experience it.

12th January, 1978

BACH CANTATA SERIES RESUMED

Brandenburg Concerto no. 1 in F
Cantata no. 208, "Was mir behagt"

One of our important annual institutions is the series of Bach cantatas which John Beckett and his friends give us each February in St Ann's. The first of this year's took place yesterday afternoon with a packed church.

For the first time we had a secular cantata in which four classical deities join to extol the virtues of Duke Christian of Saxe Weissenfels on his birthday. This is a long cantata of 15 movements, including two joyful choruses sung with brilliance and verve by the Cantata Singers. The prevailing spirit is exuberance, with a lot of floridly decorative singing, and the team of singers could not have been bettered — Irene Sandford, Violet Twomey, Frank Patterson, William Young.

In the very opening recitative, Miss Sandford seemed a scrap uncomfortable but she immediately settled in to a performance of virtuosity and joy. Indeed she and Mr Patterson sang the flourish on "zusammen" (aptly enough) at the end of the fifth number with obvious and infectious delight at their tour de force.

Violet Twomey had two arias, in both of which she was splendid and one of them was the famous "Sheep may safely graze". It was a great pleasure to hear it in context, and sung, and with its original instrumentation of two recorders (Jenny Robinson and David Agnew) and continuo. The latter were, as usual, Betty Sullivan and Gillian Smith of whom the former had a far more acrobatic part throughout the cantata than usual. William Young's two arias are both vigorous, the second also somewhat bucolic. He gave us them both in fine style (but he must not let his German pronunciation slip).

The cantata starts in praise of hunting to which the duke was addicted. It was apt, then, to precede it with the first Brandenburg concerto written for a concertino group of two hunting horns, three oboes, and violin, in which the horns used various of the actual hunting calls of Brandenburg.

I do not think I have ever heard such a spirited, authentic, stylish and entirely enjoyable performance. Mr Beckett put his concertino (Victor Malirsh, Thomas Briggs, Helmut Seeber, Lindsay Armstrong, Patricia Harrison, Mary Gallagher) in a row in front of the ripieno, with Gilbert Berg (bassoon) also in front. This resulted in a new and fresher (and also clearer) balance of sound. Also Mr Beckett had the strings of NICO using a baroque style of bowing, so different from the romantic bowing in last Thursday's concert at the Masonic Hall. Altogether it was a revelation of what this concerto should sound like and at its most pleasurable.

6th February, 1978

FIRST PERFORMANCE BY RTÉ QUARTET

Quartet no. 74 in G minor, op. 74, no. 3 — Haydn
Quartet no. 2, op. 17 — Bartók
Quartet no. 15 in A minor, op. 132 — Beethoven

The Radio Telefís Éireann Academica String Quartet (to give the group its full title) made their Dublin debut last night in the National Gallery to a packed audience who cheered them loudly at the end, a heart-warming response to a quartet that reminded me of that wonderful cycle of the Beethoven quartets that Victor Leeson presented years ago with the Aeolian Quartet.

And the new quartet deserved the applause and the cheering. In every way they are the finest quartet RTÉ has ever had and it is to be hoped that RTÉ really appreciate what they have. Cork certainly does, but RTÉ?

For once, RTÉ did set out to publicise their new group's debut in the capital to a considerable extent, as far as dailies and weeklies were concerned. But their very own organ, the *RTÉ Guide*, contained not one syllable about this important event for the future for its radio and even television subscribers. Presumably the same treatment as RTÉ accord to their RTÉSO: not by one syllable did the *Guide* tell listeners that Sunday's broadcast was of music the orchestra took so splendidly to Mainz in March. The orchestra is used to this appalling treatment. RTÉ must not let its apparent apathy discourage this splendid quartet, who are probably used to more civilised cultural treatment.

They are not only a very splendid quartet and a group of very fine string players, but in Mariana Sirbu-Dancila they have an outstanding violinist and leader. They play very much as *pares*, but she is certainly *prima*.

They all have a remarkable strength, but this extraordinary power is not at the expense of beauty of tone. They can make an electrifying attack and yet the tone still sings.

This was a most formidable programme with which to introduce themselves. Possibly it and the occasion produced some added tension. Not that that was detectable in any ordinary way, but it may have led to a strangely unsmiling and very serious interpretation of the Haydn, with everything in place (except the exposition repeat) but none of the *Gemütlichkeit* that informs nearly everything that Haydn wrote.

For Bartók, this attitude was perfect and from start to finish this was one of the most completely understanding performances of the work and of the man that I recall. When they come (as they must) to give us the complete Bartók series, that should be really wonderful.

The real test was, of course, the Beethoven and here again we had a stunning performance, with total assurance, certainty, power, perfect interchange and balance between the voices. It is possible, however, that, being still young, this splendid group have so far devoted so much of their energies to achieve the standards of a world-class quartet that they have not had time to consider all the content? This Beethoven was brilliantly lit, with light and dark but too brilliantly for half-light, and is it not in the half-lights that much of the revelation is to be found?

There is so much more to write of them, but may I now join Geraldine Neeson in her welcome to "our new friends" and tell them that we hope for years of thrilling musical experience from them?

24th May, 1978

JAMES GALWAY RETURNS TO DUBLIN

Divertimento in D, K. 136 — Mozart
Flute Concerto no. 2 in D, K. 314 — Mozart
Symphony no. 29 in A, K. 29 — Mozart
Flute Concerto in G, op. 29 — Stamitz

There was a great air of celebration and expectancy last night in St. Patrick's Cathedral before the first of the three packed-out concerts given by James Galway and the New Irish Chamber Orchestra conducted by André Prieur.

The concert started splendidly with NICO and Mr Prieur giving us a performance of the divertimento which had all the elegant sensitivity which first endeared NICO to us. So too their performance of the symphony, a popular symphony certainly but one that can be very boring unless played with the most pointed, loving and Mozartean phrasing. Last night it was a joy.

The traumatic experiences of this past year* might have had an effect on James Galway's charisma or on his playing. From last night it is a pleasure to report that his flute playing is as superb and as uniquely musical as ever. Indeed his rather naughtily, cheerful, smiling dissociation from the tutti is unchanged too, but it might well be changed.

Just what makes Jimmy's playing stand out from everyone else's is a matter of the tiniest rhythmic and tonal finesses, but they just make us know what Mozart's music is about or that the usually pedestrian music of Johann Stamitz can be fired to sound heavenly. All the magic is there still and, being able to hear him playing the ever familiar, ever beautiful "Dance of the Blessed Spirits" from Gluck's *Orphée* as an encore, I could only marvel afresh at his gift for putting so much ethereal beauty into the shaping of every phrase and every note.

1st July, 1978

* James Galway had been knocked down by a moped in Geneva.

EUROPEAN YOUTH ORCHESTRA AT THE RDS

Variations and Fugue on a Theme of Purcell, op. 34 — Britten
Prelude to Act III of La traviata — Verdi
Academic Festival Overture, op. 80 — Brahms
Symphonie fantastique, op. 14 — Berlioz

By no means all the occasions with the biggest publicity and general hoo-ha turn out to be the most worth while. It is good therefore to report that the long awaited visit by the European Community Youth Orchestra to the RDS last night was a tremendous success from the audience's point of view — and presumably for the young people themselves.

The concert was to have been conducted by Lorin Maazel. Unfortunately he had injured his leg getting out of a taxi in Munich and could not travel. As a result, the Brahms overture was substituted for the *Meistersinger* overture which several advance versions of the programme had promised us and Edward Heath came here to conduct it and the National Anthem and the so-called European Anthem. Mr Heath got splendid performances and if his left hand is not particularly expressive what should a Tory politician be doing with the left?

The rest of the concert was conducted by James Judd (with whom we are already familiar for his excellent work at the Wexford Festival). With no disrespect to Mr Maazel, we may have been the gainers. After all, Mr Judd formed the orchestra by running the auditions all over the Community and selecting all the players. He is their rehearsal and training conductor so that the big names have only been taking over someone else's work while we here were able to hear the orchestra with their own.

Certainly they responded magnificently to him and gave us an electrifying concert. Admittedly they are the cream of the Community's young musicians of the future (and unlike the NYO include professional students). Admittedly too, their strings are as many as our whole RTÉSO and they were playing without a proscenium arch.

Nonetheless they were splendid. If there were a number of little fluffs (especially in the testing Verdi) they were probably due to the effect on teenagers of a gruelling schedule — breakfast 8.30 a.m.; rehearsal at RDS 10a.m. — 1 p.m.; 1-2.15 p.m. lunch and visit the Horse Show; 2.15-4.15 p.m. sightseeing tour; 4.15 p.m. change; 6 p.m. reception at Ivy (that's what the handout called it!) House; 8 p.m. concert; 10.30 p.m. party in TCD. And this morning they check in at 6.20 a.m. at Collinstown.

With that sort of day their standard of technique, control and ensemble were marvellous.

The brilliance, atmosphere and vivacious excitement of the Britten made one wonder whether one doesn't need to be young to play his "Young Person's Guide" — quite apart from it being a virtuoso piece to display a fine orchestra.

This was, I think, the best live performance I have ever heard of the Berlioz. As well as its emotional content, the first movement had form and a detailed care for all those little unexpected nuances of Berlioz's that keep the listener on tenterhooks.

So, too, the Ball was certainly frenetic, but swung along as though really dancing. And so on to the end. That the strings had such fine and nuanced tone and real unanimity presumably came from Hugh Maguire's coaching. The players' enthusiasm, skill and youth did much of the rest, but the major credit must go to James Judd. I am glad that we, at least, were able to appreciate that.

10th August, 1978

LUCIANO PAVAROTTI RETURNS TO DUBLIN

Caro mio ben — Giordani
Che farò (Orfeo) — Gluck
Che fiero costume (Eteocle) — Legrenze
In questa tomba oscura, WoO 133 — Beethoven
Il barcaiolo — Donizetti
La danza — Rossini
Cielo e mar (La Gioconda) — Ponchielli
Benedetto sia l'giorno: Pace non trovo (Petrarch) — Liszt
Fra poco a me (Lucia) — Donizetti
Four Songs — Tosti

Before he started singing at the Gaiety Theatre, Dublin, last night, Luciano Pavarotti bade us note that the cover of his programme was black. Most of us would know why. For those who did not he wanted to say that he was dedicating last night's recital and tomorrow's to the memory of "my very, very dear friend, Bill O'Kelly".

This programme was beautifully produced with notes about the songs, original texts and translations. And it was "so arranged that, if the appropriate page is turned at the beginning of each group of songs, there should be silence until the end of the group". Congratulations to the DGOS (who presented the recital) — but the house lights were extinguished so that all their care went for naught. Perhaps tomorrow they will have the house lights up just enough for the audience to use the programme.

Luciano Pavarotti first came to Dublin in 1962 to sing in *Rigoletto*, a crucial point in his career. He came next in 1964 when he was the utterly sympathetic Alfredo to Margherita Rinaldi's first Violetta with Taddei as Germont *père*. He has not been back since.

Last night's recital was a curious mixture. On the one hand we all felt honoured to have this presently world-famous tenor in Dublin and back in Dublin. And much of what he did was certainly most beautiful, out of an interestingly cast programme which was by no means the ordinary succession of operatic arias. And yet it was not all delight. Perhaps his voice was not enjoying our bitterly cold weather, and singers are at the mercy of so much.

His opening song, the beautiful "Caro mio ben", needs perfection of the placing of the notes. Mr Pavarotti pitched his very opening note low and had to adjust it, presumably a chance misfortune. But there were too many other misfortunes in that song. Fortunately they were redeemed by exquisitely placed notes and dynamics in "Che farò", even if that was hardly 18th century in style, any more than Beethoven's aria was really his style, movingly though it was sung.

It was only with "Cielo e mar" that Mr Pavarotti moved into his own. The two Petrarch sonnets are seldom heard and it was a treat to hear them. The "Lucia" aria was fine if not show-stopping, and Tosti's songs (the "Farewell", "Aprile", "Ideale", and "Marechiare") were exactly what they should be.

And yet it was the first encore, "Una furtiva lagrima" (from Donizetti's *L'elisir*), that showed us the honeyeyed, glorious tenor we had come expecting to hear and this was capped by "Donna non vidi mai" (From Puccini's *Manon Lescaut*) and "Nessun dorma" from *Turandot*. In these three there was the true star quality.

After that last, the black curtain was shown to be a gauze behind which was the DGOS chorus, who assisted Mr Pavarotti in "Adeste fideles", and doubtless other carols after that when I had left. John Wustman was a satisfactory accompanist. I am quite sure that another 24 hours in Dublin will ensure that tomorrow night Mr Pavarotti's voice will have had all its true quality restored to it.

19th December, 1979

DANIEL BARENBOIM IN BEETHOVEN AT RDS

Sonata no. 31 in A flat, op. 110
33 Variations on a waltz by Diabelli, op. 120

Having had a permanent appointment, for however many years it has been, to hear and enjoy John Beckett's Bach cantatas at St Ann's on the first three Sunday afternoons of February, pleasures which have become a sort of national institution by now, I do not really approve of my having gone off yesterday afternoon to the RDS instead.

Dame Ruth Railton, who now lives among us, was presenting a piano recital by Daniel Barenboim, in aid of multiple sclerosis research at the Adelaide Hospital — it will be recalled that his wife, the famous cellist, Jacqueline du Pré, is a victim of the disease — and this apparently was his only free performing date this year. This was also his first visit to Ireland and it is said that, according to his present intention, it will have been his last solo recital, as he intends to concentrate almost entirely on his conducting career.

He certainly chose a formidable programme. At this moment of writing I am dismayed that my detailed recollection of the sonata (even that one!) is submerged under those of the Diabelli variations.

Some things do surface, such as the stillness of his soft playing at the beginning, the restrained tension of the Adagio-arioso, and the total essence of part playing in the fugue — a quality again and again displayed in the variations. And, once more, the stillness of the resumption of the inverted fugue.

The speed and violence of the Theme of the variations startled me. Here was no delightful little waltz, however pregnant with possibilities — would Diabelli himself not have been startled? And yet this violence expressed how Beethoven could be moved to produce this tremendous piano swan-song (and, for the matter of that, how 49 other composers produced one variation each on the tune).

I was surprised at Mr Barenboim's tendency to make everything above *mf* just about as loud as possible, and what seemed to me his misunderstanding of no. 13, at the amount of force, vehemence, violence as opposed to strength and power. On the other hand, and much more importantly, the overwhelming impression was of authority. This was one of the world's great musicians who had clearly thought long about the work and was showing us Beethoven's greatest piano work as he understood Beethoven's thought. It was a privilege to have the experience.

9th February, 1981

GREAT MUSIC PLAYED BY A GREAT ORCHESTRA AT RDS

Overture, Portsmouth Point — Walton
Variations on an Original Theme ("Enigma"), op. 36 — Elgar
Symphony no. 1 in E minor, op. 39 — Sibelius

The RDS's 250th anniversary celebrations gave Dublin (and Ireland) another fine occasion last night when the London Symphony Orchestra played to over 4,000 people in the Main Hall in Ballsbridge.

Even when the National Concert Hall is fully run in, it will presumably be too small for great foreign orchestras to visit us there — I understand that even a full house in the RDS Main Hall will barely have broken even, and therefore the 1,300-seater in Earlsfort Terrace cannot be expected to. And it cannot be too often emphasised that our national Concert Hall is needed for our own regular occasions and not for occasional spectaculars.

Whether the RDS Main Hall is to be the place for great visiting orchestras is another matter, but the RDS have put us deeply in their debt for bringing the Czech Philharmonic a couple of years ago and now the LSO. The acoustics of the Main Hall are curious. Last night, from my excellent seats, the wind sections overbalanced the magnificently united and toned strings. This gave me a remarkable view of the Elgar, as though from a wind point of view. I am delighted to have had it, especially in such a fabulous performance. In the interval I made inquiries from friends whose judgment I trust in other parts of the hall, and found that to some the strings came across magnificently, but at the expense of the wind, and that elsewhere balance was right. On balance and remembering the Czechs, I feel that perhaps the LSO's touring team may not have had as splendid a string weight as at home in London.

That, however, is less important by a long way than the sheer magnificence of the overall performance.

It was entirely right that a great British orchestra, conducted by a great Finnish conductor, Paavo Berglund, should bring two works by English composers of note and a symphony by the great Finnish composer.

Portsmouth Point is a work whose bustle, brilliance and sheer high-spirited joy is all too seldom offered. The performance captured all the brilliance so that I wanted to leave my seat and dance with it. What a band!

From this great, warm-hearted, fabulously-detailed performance of the "Enigma" variations, not only did we bask in the marvellous imagination of Elgar, but thanks to this great orchestra and Mr Berglund, we could appreciate how the work made Elgar an internationally-renowned composer before the English really took to him. There were so many sharply-illuminated details. The sense of getting into the heart of the work made me expect that suddenly, there would be revealed the solution of the Enigma, the greater, "larger theme that, never heard, goes with" Elgar's theme — not that it was. And it was brilliant as well as kind to give us the final variation, Elgar himself, as an encore at the end of the concert.

The symphony was simply great music played by a great orchestra under a great conductor. Either I settle down for a whole column to dilate on the exposure of every detail of the work and of its whole marvellous architectural shaping, or I leave it at that; which I do.

This was a triumph for the RDS — just another one. And it was also a joy to see back in Ireland Maurice Meulien (sub-leader of the cellos), Nuala Herbert (harp), Kurt Goedicke (timpanist). To see them here again is a measure of how we still miss them.

10th April, 1981

INTERLUDE

THE NATIONAL CONCERT HALL SAGA

During the 1950s the RÉSO performed in the tiny Phoenix Hall off Dame Court. Visiting orchestras and celebrities played either in the Theatre Royal in Hawkins Street, a "super-cinema" with a capacity of 3,750, or in the Adelphi Cinema in O'Connell Street which held 2,000. Dublin clearly needed a concert hall. Of all the issues that Charles Acton undertook to champion for music in Ireland, none was so intensely committed as his campaign for a concert hall worthy of a European capital and a musical nation. The following excerpts taken from the plethora of articles on this topic testify to his zeal.

A NATIONAL CONCERT HALL: DUBLIN'S PRESSING NEED
14th January, 1960

Tomorrow night at the Theatre Royal, Dublin, there is to be a concert of quite unusual importance for the future musical life of the nation and capital. The Radio Éireann Symphony Orchestra will be playing and for once we shall have some chance of hearing an orchestra in front of the proscenium.

Giaconda da Vito will be playing in Brahms's violin concerto. And it will be conducted by Tibor Paul, who in his autumn visit seemed to be outstandingly the best conductor who has worked with RÉ.

But the importance of the event is not in itself, but in its being the first shot in a campaign to get us a Concert Hall, *if we really want one.*

"If we really want one" is the crux of the matter, and tomorrow night and the next few months will show us whether we really do. Our national and municipal disgrace in being the only European nation and capital not to have a concert hall is a platitude. And there is a danger that we are so inured to it, and so accustomed to making do with unsatisfactory substitutes, that we may be too much sunk in apathy to make the personal, individual effort needed to get one. For let us make no mistake, a concert hall can only come from our personal and individual efforts.

Successive Governments and Ministers of Finance have, during four decades, paid lip-service to our need, but have always found the time not ripe or too many prior pressing necessities.

They will go on doing so until we are dead until we prove that we actively *want* a concert hall. It is no good our sitting down and saying that "They" or "the Government" should do something about it. We, as individuals, must prove the demand by the only effective means in our individual power — by actually making the personal sacrifices of putting up, if not the whole £400,000 needed, at least a very substantial part of it; the first step being, of course, a full house tomorrow night.

The sudden arrival of tomorrow's initial fund-raising concert has surprised many people who did not know what has been being going on quietly behind the scenes. This present attempt to get us a hall dates from the inception in 1947 of the Music Association of Ireland, one of whose primary aims is "to work for the establishment of a national concert hall." A committee of its council explored the situation patiently, and in 1952 a company, limited by guarantee, was incorporated, "Concert and Assembly Hall, Ltd", C.A.H. for short.

C.A.H.'s two first tasks were to assure themselves that

Radio Éireann, far and away our most important impresario, would use the new building for events that now happen in the Phoenix Hall; and to find a suitable site.

Radio Éireann were naturally co-operative. But the second task was more difficult. After many disappointments, the site is now fixed on the corner of Nicholas and High streets, diagonally opposite Christ Church Cathedral. Clearing of the site has been well started, and a lease from the City Corporation will be drawn up as soon as the site is clear.

The next steps are money and plans. C.A.H. hope that the design for the building will be a matter of international competition, which should produce a noble and impressive building. It is unusual to come before the public for money without issuing some prospectus with approximate details. C.A.H. may well be wise, since public interest and discussion may help them to give us what we want and not what some "They" may think we want.

The present proposals involve a large hall of 1,500 to 2,000 seats, a smaller hall of 500 to 600 seats, and "other rooms which can be used for rehearsals and as studios, and it is hoped that there will be a cafe or restaurant on the top floor which could be used for social occasions and dances." Presumably also provision will be made for committee and meeting rooms, office accommodation and ancillary services.

[...]

It has been obvious from the start that music alone cannot make a complete concert hall structure pay its way. But it is equally obvious that our lack of hall accommodation for conferences, both domestic and international, of all sorts is hopelessly inadequate. To no one is this clearer than to Bord Fáilte, who could make Dublin the site of far more events if we had the accommodation, especially in the summer, when there is least music.

Though this matter of tourism leads one to think that

officialdom will in fact play its part in the cost, it remains as clear as a pikestaff that the main work must come from each one of us. We shall not have a hall in our day unless tomorrow and afterwards you, who are reading this, show that *you* want a hall by actively paying for it.

TWO HEADLINES

The Irish Times, 18th January, 1964
KENNEDY MEMORIAL WILL BE CONCERT HALL IN DUBLIN
Government decision announced

Ireland's State memorial to the late John Fitzgerald Kennedy is to take the form of a concert and assembly hall to be built in Dublin and named after the late President. The Government has taken this decision on the advice of the Arts Council, it was officially announced last night.

The entire cost of the project, which has been approved by the leaders of the three main political parties, will be provided from State funds. [...]

The Irish Times, 10th March, 1965
KENNEDY MEMORIAL HALL PRIMARILY FOR MUSIC

The Kennedy Memorial Hall will not be a mere all-purpose hall in which music will occasionally be performed, said the Taoiseach, Mr Lemass, when he introduced models and designs for the memorial buildings to a large assembly of local and foreign journalists at a reception held yesterday at Iveagh House, Dublin.

THE KENNEDY HALL
3rd August, 1967

A recent leading article referred to "silence in the musical world" about the Kennedy Memorial concert hall. To the extent that there is silence in the musical world, it is the silence of hope and crossed fingers. As well as that the secretiveness and occasional soothing noises made by the Government have imposed a silence upon us.

The Minister for Finance, in answer to a question in the Dáil, only a few weeks ago (May 2nd) said that "planning was proceeding satisfactorily, but it was not possible to say when construction was likely to begin". What can one say?

The secretiveness and silence in high places is characteristic of our Government departments. The ineptitude and stupidity, with which they throttle and kill public approval of their good doings by refusing to allow the public to know what is happening, induce a sort of hopeless, numbed despair in those of us who want to cheer and encourage. [...]

THE KENNEDY HALL: DEAD OR ALIVE?
2nd January, 1974

The Kennedy Memorial Concert Hall is dead: long live the Patrick Joseph Murphy Congress Centre. I, and many thousands of other people, are ashamed that ours is the only country in Europe without any form of national concert hall, or any decent concert hall in our capital city. That we have been so ashamed for decades does not decrease the shame.

We all of us know the promises made by the Fianna Fáil Government in 1964. Within a few months of the assassination of President John F. Kennedy (which took place a decade ago) the Government of the Republic of Ireland promised to build a national concert hall in memory of that great and inspiring Irish-American. We know only too well that this has been just one more promise made by politicians and governments which has been broken.

That knowledge may be shame enough to us at home in Ireland. It is an embarrassing shame when one is in the United States of America and is asked why the Kennedy Memorial has not yet been built. It is an embarrassing shame abroad to speak against one's own Government; the most one can do is to say that we are all hoping that the present Government will honour the nation's undertaking.

I am not concerned to retrace the sad, dishonest past, but to project what one can only hope to be the honest and profitable future. Nevertheless, there are a few matters from the past which must be rehearsed, as briefly as possible, as a prelude to one's hopes for the future.

After President Kennedy's assassination, the Government of Ireland asked the Arts Council what form the national memorial to him should take. They swiftly replied "A National Concert Hall." The Government accepted the recommendation, appointed a nine-man, all-party committee of T.D.s under the chairmanship of the Minister for Finance. This committee did a considerable amount of junketing around Europe and received outstanding co-operation and assistance from the German Institute for Cultural Relations and its liaisons in Germany. As a result, within a reasonably short time, the then Taoiseach told the nation and the world that the Kennedy Memorial would be built at Beggar's Bush to designs by Raymond McGrath, senior architect of the Board of Works.

The cost was then estimated at £1m. There the matter rests — still.

I believe that we might now have this hall, already built, if it had not been for two things: what Michael Bowles has in the past called "the reticence of the civil servant," and a curious misunderstanding of function between the principal architect and Bord Fáilte.

Seán Lemass's announcement of the plans, intentions and promises stirred a great deal of public interest. The natural thing, from there on, would be to have kept the public interested in what was going on. During the next couple of years, many interesting things took place. A special office was opened in Lansdowne Road for the detailed plans and drawings. [...] Something like a quarter of a million pounds was spent by the Government, through the Board of Works, on the detailed plans for the whole thing.

I was given, at one stage, a great deal of information about all this; under strict embargo that it was not to be printed until the All-Party Committee met and authorised the information. That was 1966. I am still waiting for authorisation!

That was a characteristically Civil Service means of making sure that the public lost interest and that the whole thing went off the boil.

LIGHT AT THE END OF THE CONCERT HALL TUNNEL?
7th June, 1978

So many times have Governments cried "Wolf!" that one is very wary. Or rather, I suppose, one should rephrase it, so many, many times have Government wolves cried "Mutton, Mutton to come!"

Never mind history up to 1965. I made a right fool of myself then when I believed the solemn and ceremoniously delivered words of Sean Lemass on March 9th, 1965, when he told us that we were to have a concert hall as a memorial to President Kennedy, that January, 1966, would see the commencement of the project and autumn 1968 its completion for £1,750,000.

You and I did spend one-seventh of that sum on TDs and Board of Works architects junketing round Europe looking at concert halls, on consultancy services from Ove Arup for the steelwork, to Ralph Downes for an organ specification, for a 1:10 model made by the leading world acoustics expert, Professor Cremer of Berlin, and getting all the magnificent plans ready to go out to tender. And until Kennedy had been nearly a decade underground and the Government had changed, no Fianna Fáil Finance Minister had the common honesty to tell the punters that that money had all been thrown down the drain with nothing but bitterness to show for it.

Then in May, 1974, the Fine Gael Finance Minister summoned us to Leinster House and at that meeting we learnt that he was going to spend £750,000 on tarting up the Great Hall of UCD to make what he called a "State Concert Hall" and what we were clearly told would be nearly exclusively a desperately needed home for the RTÉSO; and that it would open its doors early in 1977. Little news has emerged since save that we learnt that a new set of Board of Works architects were travelling Europe looking at concert halls.

Now in June 1978, Pearse Wyse, TD, Minister of State in the Department of Finance, has been "delighted to have this opportunity to announce the placing of a contract for the adaptation of part of the University building at Earlsfort Terrace as a Concert Hall".

He told us that the work will be "completed in about two and a half years". That should be around January 1982 —

shall we hope for some time in 1982?

Other people, too often disappointed in the past and by now embittered, are refusing to trust the news. I am still an optimist, but so often bitten as to be very shy, and at least I hope we may believe all this news. But so often in the past governments have slid out of their undertakings when they have found a real or conveniently announced financial crisis. Can this one, or have they gone beyond the point of no return? [...]

OPENING CONCERT AT THE NATIONAL CONCERT HALL

Fortunately Caroline Walsh is writing elsewhere about the event and occasion of the State Opening of the National Concert Hall last night, for this was clearly about the most important thing to happen to music in our country for a long time, to whatever extent the Hall is what we need and whatever we may eventually decide about it.

Its qualities and capabilities are matter for discussion over the next few months at the least. Acoustically I can report that the improvement compared with the tests last July is dramatic. It is also a place where listening to music is a festive, important affair, quite apart from the glitter of a state opening. But all such important topics must be left till later. Now we are concerned with the opening concert itself, although I hope that I may be allowed to offer our congratulations to Michael O'Doherty and Alan Smith, the principal architect and the site architect; to Fred O'Donovan, the Chairman of the Board; to Lindsay Armstrong, the manager; to Gerard Victory, head of music in RTÉ; to George Waters, who had enormous technical influence; and heavens knows how many people it was that made last night's delight. Interestingly, the concert went out live on television to the USSR, the BBC, Belgium; and on radio to Yugoslavia, Belgium, Spain, Australia, Indonesia and Sri Lanka — a curious list.

The first work was Seóirse Bodley's new choral symphony, commissioned for the occasion. It set 10 newly-written poems of Brendan Kennelly.

These poems explore the nature of music and its relationship with us. They are grouped into three movements with virtually no breaks. Dr Bodley starts with a deep pedal C (which would probably be even more impressive if there were a 32-foot organ rank), and one wonders whether he had embarked on something like the beginning of *Also sprach Zarathustra*. He had not, but it is nearly as impressive.

The music is tonal. At times the chordal writing and the choral progressions shared qualities with Vaughan Williams's *Sea Symphony* — and I write that as a devotee of the latter. It could be said that Dr Bodley has written music as old-fashioned or as individual or as strange as Ó Riada's Hoelderlin songs seemed when they appeared. That is another compliment. The partnership between poet and composer is such that we need time to digest the poems and then to soak ourselves in the setting of them. It is up to RTÉ now to perform the work often enough in the next year or two for us to absorb all aspects — and preferably to issue a record as well.

Colman Pearce conducted with sympathy the RTÉSO, Our Lady's Choral Society, the RTÉ Singers and Chorus, the Choristers of St Patrick's Cathedral, Violet Twomey, Bernadette Greevy, Louis Browne and William Young, while Andreas Ó Gallchoir spoke the motto-titles of the songs most impressively. One thing very clear about the hall is that it is an excellent instrument for these four soloists.

It is absurd, of course, to write of a performance of Beethoven's choral symphony as the also ran. It was not, of course. I could argue a few points with Mr Pearce, but he and his orchestra and in the last movement his singers did give us a memorable performance that was very much *echt* Beethoven and brought across to us the spirit and sheer achievement and depth of this great work.

If music in the NCH goes on as it started, the arts in Ireland have acquired a new dimension. If I may end on a note of sadness it is that neither of President Hillery's immediate predecessors was able to perform the ceremony considering the caring energy they both put towards fostering the art of music among us.

10th September, 1981

STOCKHAUSEN BRINGS FESTIVAL TO ITS CLIMAX

The natural climax of the Dublin Festival of 20th Century Music was the performance directed by Karlheinz Stockhausen of his *Inori* on Tuesday night at the National Concert Hall. It is an exciting fact that by last Friday the entire hall had been booked out for a work and a composer that might not be regarded as generally box office. Considering the weather, it was remarkable that at least half of the ticket holders, if not more, were able to turn up.

I must admit to arriving in a cross frame of mind about the composer. He had had three full days of rehearsals with the RTÉSO. On Saturday, admittedly, only about a score had struggled in, some on foot on the ice and snow for four or five miles with instruments and Thermoses. On Sunday about 70 of the 90 players managed it: on Monday well over half. After nearly a week of rehearsals (and they probably pretty gruelling), a remarkable amount for any single work, Mr Stockhausen decided not to use the orchestra, but to use a tape instead. This seemed shabby treatment.

Before the performance he disarmed our umbrage by regretting the need to use a tape, pointing out that a tape of such a work was like experiencing a sculpture by looking at a picture postcard.

In fact, the tape was so full of much extraneous noise and crackles that I am sure that our devoted orchestra's performance would have been greatly preferable, even if it had been less than a perfect art. And from the tape I had the impression that many of the details of the score might not be ordinarily discernible anyway.

Inori lasts some 70 minutes, dates from 1974 and is for orchestra and one or (in complete unison) two dancer-mimes who perform prayer gestures.

Inori is a Japanese word meaning prayer, invocation,

adoration. The original performances were with one dancer-mime soloist, either Alain Louafi or Elizabeth Clarke. On Tuesday night both of them took part. I would have preferred Miss Clarke on her own, for two reasons. Firstly, their ensemble was far from perfect, although doubtless had we had the orchestra Mr Stockhausen would have been conducting them as much as the instrumentalists. Secondly, Miss Clarke had the detailed delicacy of gestures and hand movements of the African which made Mr Louafi's seem coarse imitations of the white man.

The work is constructed on a five-part "basic formula" which in its original form lasts about one minute. RTÉ's excellent programme booklet reproduced the schematic score of this basic formula and invited us to follow it while listening. But they turned out the house lights, so that we could not.

Though thus deprived, the whole event was a remarkable experience. Of the work's ability to grip its audience, I can testify that no one in the audience coughed during its complete duration, and there was an extraordinary atmosphere of concentrated participation.

The music is notable for remarkable concentration on single notes and on something very near to tunes at times. It is, perhaps not so much a piece of music as a ritual in music. It was certainly a very impressive aural and visual experience and, even in partial form, a climactic end to the festival as much as the *Turangalîla* Symphony was to the one at which Messiaen honoured us.

At its end, Mr Stockhausen said "It would be wonderful to come back soon and hear *Inori* with your orchestra," and he went on to describe some of the visual effects which he had written for the orchestra, bowing patterns coinciding with the soloists' gestures, and so on. And he graciously thanked the many members of the RTÉSO who had come in to hear the work. Then he gave us "as a present" a performance of the "Aries" movement from his *Sirius* (1974-1978) for electronic tape and trumpet, the latter being played by his 17-year-old son, Markus Stockhausen. The latter gave an outstanding virtuoso performance of exciting and strange music.

14th January, 1982

ALFRED BRENDEL RECITAL AT NATIONAL CONCERT HALL

Sonata in D minor, Hob 51 — Haydn
Sonata no. 8 in A minor, 310 — Mozart
Sonata no. 10 in A, 664 — Schubert
Sonata, op. 1 — Berg
Fantasy in C, op. 17 — Schumann

The National Concert Hall last Thursday night promoted a piano recital by Alfred Brendel and, judging by the distribution of the number of empty seats, they failed in their publicity rather than suffered the misfortunes of the weather.

Alfred Brendel, then as now one of the world's great musicians, appeared here once before, at the RDS in 1966. Then, most sadly, I found that his recital had everything in place but lacked in the magic of communication. I am sure that this was a matter of the off-day that even the greatest musicians can have. There was no such question on Thursday night.

On the other hand, for all the perfection of his playing of the first two sonatas, I wondered why I was not "sent", even though they were in totally right style, with the expectedly great intellectual commitment (his treatment of repeats was interesting and I am sure that he could easily have justified each). I concluded that this was a matter of the difference between the live and the recorded performance.

The latter has to have a restraint and fidelity so that one is as pleased and understanding at the hundredth performance as at the first, whereas, live, the artist can point details, as though to say: "This is the only time you will hear this from me: listen to it!"

Thus the searing first movement of the Mozart would have been a splendid recording, and the fantasy-like emotionalism of that slow movement was not put across with the intention of gripping us then and once and for all, in spite of the marvellously balanced and judged phrasing of the whole thing.

The Schubert was a different matter, since Mr Brendel conveyed both the melting loveliness of every theme, every phrase, and also the shape of the movements in such a way as to show how utterly right Schubert was.

In the Berg sonata, Mr Brendel was less concerned with revealing the intellectual certainty of Berg's sonata form than with making us aware of the deep feelings and emotionalism of Berg's creation and the sheer beauty of the music.

All of this was leading to the most complete and wonderful performance of the Schumann Fantasy that I have ever heard or hope to hear. Mr Brendel is one of the supremely intellectual and understanding of the world's great pianists, but here he left all that behind, as something passed through. Here was the music, the composer's feelings and creation as he obviously wanted us to hear them. Schumann must always sing: he did. Schumann runs through a great variety of emotions: Mr Brendel made him. How marvellous was the excitement of the "con energia" movement, and the succeeding arpeggios of the "Lento sostenuto" start! But I could easily go on pointing to details that made up the fabulous insight and communication of this wonderful performance.

It is not my place to write about encores, and after the extraordinary experience of the Schumann I did not want anything else. I was, however, drawn to hearing it, a Bach-Busoni chorale prelude, played with such wisdom and meditation that it set the seal on a great experience.

18th January, 1982

JÁNOS FÜRST AND SUZANNE MURPHY TRIUMPH IN MOZART

Symphony no. 29 in A, K. 201
Non temer, K. 490
Nehmt meinen Dank, K. 383
Non mi dir (from Don Giovanni)
Symphony no. 33 in B flat, K. 319

On Saturday night the National Concert Hall was understandably packed for the concert by the New Irish Chamber Orchestra, at which János Fürst conducted and Suzanne Murphy was the soloist, not only her first appearance here since her triumph with Welsh National Opera in London in *I puritani*, but her only appearance for about two years (when she triumphed in Handel).

Naturally, it was another triumph. How glorious her voice now is! It filled the Concert Hall effortlessly, as would that of any of the world's singers. And her Mozart style was as impeccable as her Handel had been — although I would have thought that one or other (or both) of the last two *fermate* in *Nehmt meinen Dank* should have had a sizeable embellishment as a lead in to the following passages; and I am quite sure that Aloysia Lange took the opportunity offered.

I am also quite sure that Aloysia would never have had a music stand in front of her. Like Miss Murphy, she was a great opera singer and would have let nothing come between her and her audience.

I know that others as well felt that she gave too much attention to her music and her music stand. *Non temer* was composed for insertion into *Idomeneo*. *Non mi dir* is Donna Anna's highlight in *Don Giovanni*. As an opera star, Miss Murphy had no excuse for slightly diminishing her magnificent performance in this way.

As for *Non mi dir* itself, it just made me long to attend her performance of *Don Giovanni* and to hear her recording of the opera — how soon will one of the gramophone majors engage her for one of their prestigious recordings? She deserves it and they would benefit.

As always, János Fürst gave her a perfect accompaniment.

In the two symphonies he showed us, again, just why his original Irish Chamber Orchestra still lives so excitingly in our memories. K 201, for all its great popularity, needs a special performance (and conductor) really to come off. Mr Fürst got one. From the very beginning the string tone was so silky and the first (as every) phrase so perfectly elegant and pointed. We heard the exact appreciation of piano and pianissimo, and the whole was with every strand of the music so perfectly clear and perfectly balanced so that the whole symphony became a marvellous experience.

In this symphony and in No. 33, Mr Fürst and NICO played not only what Mozart wrote, with exact attention to what Mozart did write, but they also included what one realised in these performances Mozart had implied in his writing, without ever either exceeding or contradicting the composer.

One hears such performances seldom. When one does, one can only be profoundly grateful.

28th June, 1982

MAHLER'S THIRD SYMPHONY FROM RTÉSO

Our first performance of Mahler's third symphony had to be a great occasion. And on Friday night at the National Concert Hall with Colman Pearce conducting the RTÉSO, 60 women of the Guinness Choir, the Palestrina Choir and Bernadette Greevy to a packed house, it certainly was.

A visiting orchestra (with those local singers) could have put it on in the Main Hall of the RDS, as could have our own, but the Concert Hall certainly has a magic of its own in spite of the relatively small size. And one can be overwhelmed there by such a great work with an effect entirely different from any kind of mechanical reproduction.

So it was this time. Notwithstanding what Mahler said about tradition, the tradition of having the interval after the very long first movement is one that deserves to be followed, as it was. The interval consolidates the foundation of the first movement.

Notwithstanding all the singers and their excellent performance, as they only appear in one relatively short movement, they are almost incidental. As soloist with them, Bernadette Greevy was singing in totally splendid voice as a sung declamation. I wondered that she did not observe the composer's dynamic markings, but I loved the sound she made.

The orchestra was augmented for this occasion to 94 players on the platform with three players off stage. I feel that it was mean of RTÉ only to print the names of their permanent members in the programme rather than those of everyone — it is unfair to the additional players and inadequate in giving information to the audience. Especially unfair was it to omit the name of the offstage posthorn soloist who, after all, has just as important a part as the vocal soloist's (and probably a more difficult one). It was beautifully played by Graham Hastings, who gave me one of the major pleasures of the night.

At my first live hearing and in our own Concert Hall, it was the total effect that made me spellbound. There may well have been defects in some passages. Mr Pearce may well have been going for overall effect. Never mind any such matters, it was a truly great occasion at which I am thrilled to have been present.

11th October, 1982

OUTSTANDING CONCERT WITH RTÉSO

Piano Concerto no. 5 in E flat, op. 73 — Beethoven
The Planets, op. 32 — Holst

Either I was in a highly emotional state last night or the RTÉSO concert at the National Concert Hall was a most unusually fine musical experience. I prefer to believe the latter.

Over and over again I feel that Beethoven composed his five piano concertos in such a way that the soloist has only to do what Beethoven wrote and there it is, and I find myself hard put to write anything about the soloists that is not just in the score. Especially so of the "Emperor", that most wonderful of piano concertos.

Stephen Bishop-Kovacevich was the soloist, and I do not think I have ever heard a performance to equal his. Every pianist can make a lot of the three opening flourishes, but we heard his mettle in the final forte chord that offers the orchestra the first subject. His absolutely delicious rubato around bar 160, the tumult around bar 190, the breathtaking piano-crescendo from bar 264, the fantastically dramatic diminuendo in the cadenza: all these details and so much more showed us a performance of extraordinary stature.

The fantasy of the slow movement was breathtaking, and that magical transition into the rondo was never more magical. Mr Bishop-Kovacevich showed us supremely why this has been nicknamed the Emperor of concertos.

Colman Pearce was conducting and he and the RTÉSO achieved such a complete partnership with the soloist that everyone deserves the highest possible praise — and in that context I still must praise David Carmody's horn-playing.

I may well be wrong, but I only recall one other performance of the complete *Planets* here in the last 30 years, in the Gaiety and conducted also by Mr Pearce. Though he then conducted without a score, I did not feel that he really knew his work and, of course, the proscenium arch deprived us of so much of Holst's staggering scoring.

On this occasion it was marvellous to hear the miraculous detail of the work. Mr Pearce knows the measure of the hall; and the RTÉSO, individually and collectively, have never sounded as well. And not only does Mr Pearce now know the work intimately and fully, but he communicated its spirit, its detail, its overall genius as I have never heard it before — and I thought that I really knew it already.

I have one sad complaint, that the Ladies of the Park Singers could not hold their pitch for their few bars at the end of "Neptune", and I very much hope that those of the UCC Choir will do so tonight at Cork City Hall.

I would like a whole column to write about this performance, which I saw through a haze of tears of emotion and beauty while hearing a wonderful experience. "Mars" was composed in 1913, before the world war. Mr Pearce and the RTÉSO gave us a performance of such universality that, surely, had President Reagan and Mr Andropov been in the National Concert Hall, they would have had to agree to destroy all their nuclear arms.

Saturn is "the Bringer of Old Age", but who wants old age? What we heard was such a bringer of the comfort of death that this listener felt "half in love with easeful death". What a magician Uranus was! And, even if some of the playing was more than pianissimo, Neptune brought the total mystical surrender.

If I were to die now, this concert would be a satisfying *Nunc dimittis* and it is certainly the finest thing that I have heard from Colman Pearce. My thanks to him!

20th January, 1983

SMETANA QUARTET'S SECOND CONCERT AT THE RDS

Quartet no. 10 in E flat, D.87 — Schubert
Quartet no. 1 in E minor, "From my Life" — Smetana
Quartet no. 2, "Intimate Letters" — Janáček

When the Smetana Quartet first came to the RDS, I wished that I could have demanded a third of a column of blank space in this paper and in it have written "This is the perfection of quartet playing: will readers please fill up this space with all the superlatives that they can command." That was not, of course, practical then any more than it is now. But my feelings are the same now as then, although the additional years have deepened them.

They made Schubert's youthful work have far more substance than I had ever thought it could have.

From its tremulando beginning and magnificent viola tune to its final tragic intimations, Smetana's autobiographical work was just as marvellous as it has ever been in their hands, and Janáček's avowal of his late love affair was both as moving and wonderful a string quartet as it has ever been.

To describe their playing would either be impossible, or would require at least a whole column. Let one just sum it up that, if this really is their last tour, those of us who have heard them have an imperishable memory of the peak of quartet playing. But one must hope that they will return. Either way, they leave us with our heartfelt gratitude.

15th April, 1983

USSR ORCHESTRA'S FIRST VISIT TO IRELAND

Classical Symphony in D, op. 25 — Prokofiev
Violin Concerto in D, op. 35 — Tchaikowsky
Symphony no. 6 in B minor, op. 74 — Tchaikowsky

Let us praise the National Concert Hall and Lord Killanin (as chairman of Lombard and Ulster Banking, Ireland) for presenting to us last night the USSR Symphony Orchestra, whose visit has been a great expectation for nearly half a year, and who are the first world-famous orchestra to come to our National Concert Hall. The visit was even going to bring to the Concert Hall our Taoiseach and Tánaiste, who, as far as I know, have never encouraged their own orchestra by a visit — but, in the event, they both found reasons for absence.

The cards seemed to be stacked against the orchestra. They arrived tired after being delayed by snow at Moscow. Their principal conductor, Yevgeny Svetlanov, who was to have conducted last night, had a heart attack on Sunday in Moscow so that Arvid Yansons, who was to have alternated with him on the tour, is conducting everything.

Our own orchestra numbers about 60 to 70. The USSR one numbers 120 and the sheer weight of tone from such numbers had to be a thrilling sound in our concert hall. Sadly, that seemed to me the limit of what we had.

I can only put it down to tiredness that Mr Yansons and this great orchestra gave us performances in the two symphonies that neither reached the real joy of the Prokofiev nor plumbed the depths of Tchaikowsky's last symphony. Admittedly, there was a real, tragic thrill in the start of the finale and in the resolution of that tune when it comes to be played straightforwardly and not divided contortedly between the violin sections — with such a weight of strings it had to be marvellous.

Otherwise, what should have been the concert of the decade was disappointing. Even the soloist, Valery Klimov, seemed affected, since it was no outstanding performance of the concerto, for all his warm tone and technical mastery.

Presumably it is too much to expect that they will return, and under happier circumstances. If only they would, because one was tantalised by having one of the world's famous orchestras in our own city and hall, and yet so clearly not able to give us the great performances to which their own audiences are accustomed.

15th November, 1983

BARRY DOUGLAS AT CONCERT HALL

Sonata no. 31 in A flat, op. 110 — Beethoven
Scherzo no. 3 in C sharp minor, op. 39; Nocturnes Nos. 17 in B, op. 62, no. 1 and 19 in E minor, op. 72, no. 1; Scherzo no. 4 in E, op. 54 — Chopin
Pictures at an Exhibition — Mussorgsky

There are going to be a lot of people deservedly annoyed with themselves for not being at the National Concert Hall last night for the first performance in Dublin of perhaps the most outstanding pianist to have come out of Ireland in my listening lifetime, and perhaps the finest pianist we have heard in our National Concert Hall.

Barry Douglas was born in Northern Ireland in 1960. All too often one regrets that young pianists will perform the last three of Beethoven's sonatas. No such doubts were possible on this occasion.

Mr Douglas is, like Beethoven himself, a master of legato and cantabile. He is also, to an extraordinary degree, a master of the softest-possible playing. When Beethoven marks sustained softness (as at the start of this sonata or in the adagio or the first 18 bars of the fugue), Barry Douglas sustains as few pianists do. Such intensity did he generate that throughout his playing of the first half of the concert there was not one cough during the music.

One felt that Barry Douglas had approached this great work first of all noting every single one of Beethoven's marks, including those that the composer did not write; that he then, even at 24, had worked successfully to understand all that the composer thought and felt; that he then felt as Beethoven felt and finally conveyed it to us.

Lovely though his Chopin was, either the sonata had been too cathartic for me to take anything else without an interval, or perhaps he did not fully appreciate that with Chopin the order must be changed so that one feels, adapts the music to the feeling and only then brings the intellect into play.

In the Mussorgsky, the approach was again different. Though, of course, he had never seen the pictures themselves, he imagined them so clearly that he made us see them in all their different characters, especially with a quirky humour in the chattering in Limoges market, or the chicks dancing in their shells.

Fascinating as his technical mastery is, that is a matter for piano players and teachers to watch and study. It is what he built in this remarkable recital that must stay in the memory; and especially that performance of the Beethoven.

25th May, 1984

VIENNA PHILHARMONIC AT NCH

Symphony no. 29 in A, K. 201 — Mozart
The Firebird (2nd Suite, 1919) — Stravinsky
Symphony no. 1 in C minor, op. 68 — Brahms

If Fred O'Donovan is considering engaging the Vienna Philharmonic Orchestra as the resident band of the National Concert Hall, I would say no word against the idea after (or even before) their stunning performance there last night, their second visit to Ireland, the first having been to Cork and Limerick 29 years ago.

First, however, may I praise and thank RTÉ, who were televising the event, and (I understand) Louis Lentin, for marvellously sensitive work. He did, I think, have shots of the audience, but I at least never felt subject to third-degree lights. He had at least four cameras working, but they were remarkably still (at least as far as my sightlines were concerned). Their operators were in black-tie evening dress and therefore fitted in with the remarkable occasion. If Mr Lentin can arrange television so unobtrusively, let him do lots of it! And I hope that Alpho O'Reilly took no exception to the fascia behind the orchestra naming the bank as Lombard and Ulster Banking, who were probably paying about £20 a seat (and they not cheap) so that those who got first into the queue could have this great experience.

Lorin Maazel played the Mozart symphony with 32 strings. Fair enough, and while his style was neither particularly rococo or Mozart (and he is another one who has not sufficient confidence in Mozart to observe his repeat marks), the sheer volume and attack and tone of these 32 were more than so many orchestras of twice the size.

In that Mozart, in the Stravinsky and in the symphony, in their various terms, we really heard the fabulous VPO sound — and we also heard the sound deficiencies of the NCH. The VPO sound is unique in the world, and how thrilling it was to hear it, but I am afraid that the NCH's curious acoustics impinged upon it.

Lorin Maazel made the Firebird suite at least as excitingly dramatic as it must be, with striking flashes of colour from all sections of his great orchestra.

It was extraordinary to hear this symphony twice within a couple of weeks, first from our own band under Colman Pearce, and now from Maazel and the VPO. I would not dream of analysing the difference, and I know that our own band (at about two-thirds the strength) would not regard themselves as the VPO's equals. But, while the VPO's sound was only superlative, and something to savour for the next 30 years till they return, I felt that Mr Maazel encouraged them to give us their own gorgeous sound throughout (and how marvellous it is!), but not necessarily a great interpretation of this majestically tragic symphony.

We were honoured with two encores. Beethoven's *Leonore No. 3* overture, whose performance showed, firstly and emphatically, Brahms's enormous debt to Beethoven, and secondly the folly of incorporating this whole narration of the opera in a performance of *Fidelio*.

The second was the overture to *Die Fledermaus*, which

showed us Mr Maazel as a Fred Astaire of the rostrum, and the VPO, to our laughing delight, as the superb Viennese musicians that we know they are.

To the NCH, to Lombard and Ulster, to Louis Lentin, to Lorin Maazel and, above all, to what is still probably the world's greatest orchestra, or at least that one with its uniquely lovely sound, all gratitude. May it be much less than 29 years before they return, please.

29th March, 1985

JOHN O'CONOR COMPLETES BEETHOVEN CYCLE

Sonata no. 30 in E, op. 109
Sonata no. 31 in A flat, op. 110
Sonata no. 32 in C minor, op. 111

A whole column is needed for John O'Conor's final recital of the complete piano sonatas of Beethoven in the National Concert Hall, which happened on Saturday.

I doubt if any Irish pianist has ever performed them all, as a series, anywhere, in the 163 years since they were completed.

I am sure that John Field would not have. I am equally sure that neither Hamilton Harty nor Rhona Marshall did, although they are the two Irish pianists that cross my mind as well able to. Who else?

Standing ovations are fashionable clichés elsewhere, whipped up by fans. Virtually all here (and not only factional) have been organised since we stood for Stravinsky's entry into the Adelphi. But on Saturday night it really was spontaneous, and even I, who normally take a dim view of such demonstrations, was proud to stand to applaud O'Conor.

Only once before have I heard these three sonatas in one programme and I didn't believe it could be done — from Jacques Klein on his first visit to the RDS. Such a programme must be an almost impossible task, but O'Conor succeeded.

In Opus 109 was he still in the shadow of the *Hammerklavier?* — or of the back pains that put him to bed and forced him to postpone his Limerick recital? Was that why the middle movement lacked bite? Or was it just that with these three sonatas he was seeing a whole perspective?

Anyway, in its first movement the utmost *dolce* delicacy and the *espressivo* quality of the alternating adagio passages was an illustration of all that one has read about Beethoven's own playing — the *legato*, the concentrated singing quality, the inner parts, the expression, the *Empfindung.*

And in Opus 109's finale Mr O'Conor once again showed us how variation took over Beethoven's thought and feeling towards the end.

In the first movement of Opus 110 the thought was paramount in this virtual fantasia. If its scherzo had more continuity of melody than of explosive drama, Mr O'Conor may well have been right.

While those famous crescendo chords between the forward statement and then the inversion of the finale fugue were beautifully managed, the two parts of the fugue were played with an interesting restraint, so that I felt that Mr O'Conor was revealing Beethoven the thinker, the "poet in sound" as he called himself, at the expense of the usual extrovert drama.

Leading presumably to Opus 111, with its truly majestic introduction, where we heard Beethoven's demolishing combination of sonata form and fugue, followed by that ethereal set of variations.

John O'Conor did at least three things in that sonata. He played the music with enormous dignity — which was Beethoven's. He played with a wonderful stillness. This was not O'Conor, but Beethoven. And in this dignity and stillness one could only weep with the beauty and other-worldliness of that last movement, which surely can only be described by Yeats's phrase "the trembling of the veil".

29th April, 1985

President Patrick Hillery with Charles Acton in the Hewson Room of the Royal Irish Academy of Music, where the President presented Acton with a fellowship of the RIAM. November 1990. (Photograph by Frank Miller)

INDEX

A

Acton, Carol, 10
Acton, Charles, 9–14; criticised, 93, 96–7, 100–1; discursive rhetoric, 12–13; euphemism, dislike of, 102, 103; interment, 97, 98; as musician, 96–7; national concert hall campaign, 12, 13, 151–9; newspaper articles, 13; reviewing technique, 11–13
'Acton Collection,' 13
Addison (US composer), 71–2
Adelaide Hospital, Dublin, 147
Adelphi Cinema, Dublin, 67, 69, 70, 83, 86, 87, 151, 177
Aeolian Quartet, 75–6, 140
ageism, 101
Agnew, David, 139
Agnew, Jennifer, 47
Albeniz, Isaac, 32
Albert, Prince Consort, 79
Andersson, Franz, 51
Andropov, Yuri, 170
Argo records, 78
Armstrong, Lindsay, 139, 159
Armstrong, Louis, 87, 88
Arnold, Malcolm: Toy Symphony, 74
artist-critic relationship, 22–5
artists: foreign, 19; front-ranking, 19–20; identity with composer, 28–9; insulted, 101; personal circumstances, 26–7
Arts Council, 156; funding, 12, 13
Arup, Ove, 158
Ashkenazy, Vladimir, 64–5
audience behaviour, 12, 43, 44, 101–2
audiences: exclusiveness, 26

B

Bach, Johann Sebastian, 32; Brandenburg concerto no 1, 139; Cantata no 208, 138–9; Cantatas, 138, 147; French suite no 2, 113; Fugues, 108; Prelude and fugue in C sharp, 137; *Von Himmel hoch*, 68
Bacharach, Burt, 83
Baker, Janet, 117–19
balance: in criticism, 18, 28
Balkwill, Bryan, 47
Bamberg Symphony Orchestra, 41–2
Bannister, George, 117
Barber, Samuel: Adagio, 43
Barbirolli, Sir John, 44–5, 78
Barenboim, Daniel, 147–8
Barklie, Barbara, 33
Barror, Ethna, 125
Barry, Edmund, 82
Barshai, Rudolf, 122
Barth, Herr, 49
Bartók, Béla: Quartet no 2, 141
Bayreuth, *Festspielhaus*, 49–50

181

Bayreuth Festival, 39, 48–52
BBC Symphony Orchestra, 34–5
Beckett, John, 138–9, 147
Beecham, Sir Thomas, 24, 61
Beecher, Franny, 40
Beethoven, Ludwig van, 178, 179; Cello sonata no 3, 85; Creatures of Prometheus, 113; Diabelli variations, 114, 148; Egmont overture, 43; Leonore no 3 overture, 176; Piano concertos, 169; Piano concerto no 3, 136; Piano concerto no 5 'Emperor,' 169–70; Piano sonata no 23, 111–12; Piano sonata no 30, 178; Piano sonata no 31, 148, 174, 178; Piano sonata no 32, 178–9; Quartet no 14, 75; Quartet no 15, 141; String trios, 108; Symphony no 3, 'Eroica,' 41, 89, 113; Symphony no 4, 60; Symphony no 5, 95; Symphony no 6 'Pastoral,' 132; Symphony no 7, 70, 89; Symphony no 8, 89; Symphony no 9 'Choral,' 89, 161; Trio no 2, 108; 15 Variations and fugue in E flat, 113–14; Violin concerto in D, 43; Violin sonata no 9, 55–6
Beggar's Bush, Dublin, 156
Beirer, Hans, 51
Beit, Sir Alfred, 92
Belfast Festival, 113
Bell, Donald, 66
Bellini, Vincenzo: *Puritani, I*, 166
Bello, Luigi, 54
Berg, Alban: Piano sonata, 165
Berg, Gilbert, 139
Berglund, Paavo, 150
Berlioz, Hector: Requiem, 57–9; *Symphonie fantastique*, 144; Trojans, The, 118
Bettrami, Aureliana, 54
Bishop-Kovacevich, Stephan, 84, 85, 169–70
Bloch, Ernest: *Nigun*, 55
Blood-Smyth, Shirley, 128
Bodley, Seóirse: Choral symphony, 160
Bollinger, Anne, 46
Bord Fáilte, 153
Borge, Victor, 87–8
Borsò, Umberto, 54
Boschi, Ezio, 54
Boston Symphony Orchestra, 27, 34–6, 41, 93
Boult, Sir Adrian, 9
Bowles, Michael, 157
Boydell, Barra, 123
Boydell, Brian, 10, 17, 117; Triple Concerto, 74
Boydell, Mary, 117
Brahms, Johannes: Academic Festival Overture, 9–10; Cello sonata no 2, 84–5; Piano pieces, 106; Songs, 63; Symphony no 1, 176; Variations on a Theme by Handel, 105; Violin concerto, 151
Branagan, Alfred, 82
Brendel, Alfred, 164–6
Brien, Tilla, 39
Briggs, Thomas, 139
British Council, 137
Britten, Benjamin: Folksongs, 57; Serenade for tenor, horn and strings, 122; Variations and fugue on a theme of Purcell, 144; War Requiem, 65–7
Brivkalne, Paula, 39
Browne, Louis, 160
Buckingham Palace, 79
Byrne, Gay, 133

C

Cage, John, 9
CAH, *see:* Concert and Assembly Hall Ltd
Campbell, David, 137
Campoli, Alfredo, 96

Caramia, Giacinto, 107
Carmody, David, 170
Carmody, Honor, 123
Carr, Clive, 126
Carroll, Lewis, 87
"C.A.",*see:* Acton, Charles
Castelnuovo-Tedesco, Mario, 32
Chaloner, Enid, 117
chamber groups, 107
Chardin, designer, 131
choirs, weaknesses, 34
Chopin, Frédéric, 37, 110, 174; Piano sonata no 2, 86; Twelve studies, 64–5
Christ Church Cathedral, Dublin, 126, 127
Christian, Duke of Saxe-Weissenfels, 138
cinemas, National Anthem at, 77–8
City of Birmingham Symphony Orchestra, 9
Clancy, Paddy, *30*
Clarke, Elizabeth, 163
Cliburn, Van, 69–70
community, of music, 26
comparison: criticism and, 25
composer: artist's identity with, 28–9
composers, Irish, 24
Concert and Assembly Hall Ltd (CAH), 152–3
concert hall: economics of, 134, 149, 153–4
concert programmes: collection, 13; cost, 42, 61, 72; information given, 168; misprints, 98
concerts: National Anthem at, 77, 78–9
continuity: in criticism, 18, 19, 26
Cook, Thomas & Sons, 10
Cooper, Cáit, 125
Cooper, Richard, 117, 125, 133
Cork, 61, 78, 140, 170; Vienna Philharmonic Orchestra in, 35, 36, 175
correctness: political, 102–3
correspondence, 93–103
Cosgrove, Anne, 82
Costello, Theresa, 128
coughing: inconsequential, 102
coughing during performances, 12, 32, 43, 101–2; absence of, 163
Coventry, Cathedral, 95
Craft, Robert, 67–8
Cremer, Professor, 158
criticism: and comparison, 25; continuity in, 18, 19, 26, 28; conventions of, 25; difficulties of, 28–9; in Dublin, 27–8; and enjoyment, 20–1; friendship and, 28; honest, 27–8; invited, 21; necessary skills of, 97; as opinion, 15–17; standards of, 100, 106–7; standard-setting, 18–22; worth, 16
critic-performer relationship, 22–5
critics: age, 101; editors and, 16; ill-informed, 26–7; influence, 28; mood, 29; personality, 17; responsibility, 17–18
Critic's Creed, A (talk), 13, 15–29
Croke Park, Dublin, 58, 59
Croker, June, 125, 133–4
Culwick Choral Society, 66
Curragh camp, 78
Czech Philharmonic Orchestra, 134, 135–6, 149

D

Daily Mirror, 17
Dalton, Joseph, 125
Dartington Quartet, 76
Davies, Peter Maxwell, 137–8; Miss Donnithorne's Maggot, 137–8; Stedman Doubles, 137
Debussy, Claude, 110; Cello sonata in D minor, 85

183

Deegan, Paul, 128
Dempsey, Martin, 46
Dervan, Michael, 9, 12
diction: singer's, 62, 82
Dietrich, Marlene, 83, 87
'Do-it-yourself' Messiah, 133–4
Donizetti, Gaetano: *Elisir d'amore, L,'* 146
Douglas, Barry, 173–5
Dowd, Ronald, 45
Dowland Consort, 114–17
Downes, Ralph, 158
Doyle, Col J M, 78
D'Oyly Carte Opera Company, 82
du Pré, Jacqueline, 84–5, 147
Dublin: criticism, 27–8; Promenade concerts, 61
Dublin Festival of 20th Century Music, 137, 162
Dublin Grand Opera Society, 13, 39, 46–7, 53–4, 146; chorus, 147
Dublin Music Festival, 20, 57–8
Dublin Orchestral Players, 9, 10, 101
Dublin Theatre Festival, 126
Dún Laoghaire Arts Week, 100
Dunne, Frank, 125, 128
Dutoit, Charles, 129, 130
Dvoràk, Antonin: Cello concerto, 80; Symphony no 9 'New World,' 90

E

Earlsfort Terrace, Dublin, 149, 158
Easons, book-sellers, 13
eating,: during performances, 12
Edinburgh International Festival, 20
editors: and critics, 16
Éire-Ireland, 13
Electricity Supply Board (ESB): offices, 95
Elgar, Sir Edward: Dream of Gerontius, 10, 44–5; 'Enigma' variations, 149
Emmerson, Michael, 106
encores: reviewing, 11–12
encores,: critics and, 166
encouragement: critical duty of, 18, 21, 22–5
Encyclopaedia Britannica, 10
English Language Institute, 122
enjoyment: criticism and, 20–1
errors, critical, 98–9
ESB, *see* Electricity Supply Board
Essen Opera, 38–9
European Anthem, 143
European Community Youth Orchestra, 143–5
Eurovision Song Contest, 120–1
Evangelist, The (Thompson), 125
Evans, Geraint, 46
exclusiveness, musical, 26

F

Falla, Manuel, 63
Fauré, Gabriel, 63
Feasta, 13
Feis Ceoil, 13
Ferroni, designer, 53
Festival Theatre, Cambridge, 50
Fianna Fáil party, 155, 156–7, 158
Field, John, 177
films: National Anthem following, 77–8
Fine Gael party, 158
Fires of London, The, 136–8
First World War, 77
Fishamble Street, Dublin, 69
Fitzgibbon, Edwin, 89
Fleischmann, Aloys, 78
Flitscher, Herbert, 39
foreign performers: and critical standards, 19
Forrest, Edith, 128
Frémaux, Louis, 58
Frewen, Maura, 125

friendship and: criticism, 28
Fürst, János, 71, 72, 73, 166, 167

G

Gaiety Theatre, Dublin, 38, 41, 46, 55, 59, 61, 80, 81, 96, 145, 170
Galileo, V., 32
Gallagher, David, 60
Gallagher, Mary, 123, 139
Galway, James, 11–12, 142–3
Gate Theatre, Dublin, 13, 15
Geminiani, Francesco, 71
genres: critical mastery, 26
German Institute, Dublin, 9, 105, 156
Gesualdo, Carlo, 115
Gilbert, W S, 81
Giordano, Umberto: *Caro mio ben*, 146
Giuranna, Bruno, 107
Gluck, Christoph, 56, 57; *Orphée*, 142, 146
Glynne, Howell, 46
Goddard, Scott, 27
Goedicke, Kurt, 150
Goodman, Benny, Sextette, 40
Gounod, Charles: *Ave Maria*, 37
GPA Dublin International Piano Competition, 13
Grace, Princess of Monaco, 59
Grafton Cinema, Dublin, 73
Granados, Enrique, 57
Gray, Harold, 89
Gray, Terence, 50
Greene, Plunket, 90
Greevy, Bernadette 56–7, 89, 126, 160, 168
Grieg, Edvard: Piano Concerto, 74
Groocock, Joseph, 11, 33, 34
Groocock, Richard, 74
Guinness Choir, 71, 125, 168
guitar music, 32
Gulli, Franco, 107

H

Haley, Bill and the Comets, 40–1
Hall, Dorothy, 33
Hallé Orchestra, 78
Hambourg, Leonid, 88
Hamburg Philharmonic State Orchestra, 59–60
Handel, George Frederick, 69, 118, 166; *Messiah*, 32–4, 90, 133–4, 135
Hanson, Howard: Elegy, 35
Harper, Heather, 66
Harrison, Patricia, 139
Hartleb, Hans, 39
Harty, Sir Hamilton, 177
Hastings, Graham, 169
Haydn, Joseph, 67; Quartet in E flat, 75; Quartet no 74, 141; Symphony no 83, 129
Heath, Edward, 143
Herbert, Nuala, 150
Herincx, Raimund, 126
Hewson, Heather, 82
Hibernian Hotel, Dublin, 56, 108, 111
Hillery, Patrick, 161, *180*
Hindemith, Paul: Symphony, *Mathis der Maler*, 41
Hines, Jerome, 52
Hitler, Adolf, 49
Hoffman, Grace, 51
Holst, Gustave: Planets, The, 170–1
Hopkins, Antony, 74
Hough, Fionnuala, 82
Howes, Frank, 16
Howitt, Barbara, 46

I

'I': used in criticism, 16–17
identity,: performer with composer, 28–9
impresarios,: critics and, 25

185

inconsequential coughing, 102
influence: of critics, 28
Ireland: composers, 24–5; music in, 22
Irish Army Band, 77
Irish Chamber Orchestra, 71–3, 73
'Irish Heritage Series,' 13
Irish Music and Musicians (Acton), 13
Irish National Anthem, 77, 78–9, 143; style, 78
Irish National Ballet, 53–4
Irish National Gallery, 140
Irish Opera Group, 73
Irish Times, The, 9, 11, 15, 16, 17
Irish traditional music, 13
Iron Acton, Bristol, 9
Italian String Trio, 107–8
Iturbi, José, 96

J

Janácek, Leos: Quartet no 2 'Intimate Letters,' 172
Johnson, Samuel, 26
Johnston, David, 126
Judd, James, 143–4, 145
judgment: informed, 20

K

Kalman, Arthur, Productions, 73
Katchen, Julius, 105–6
Keilberth, Joseph, 42
Kelly, Séamus, 101, 102
Kennedy, John Fitzgerald, 156, 158
Kennedy Memorial Hall: plans for, 89, 154–8
Kennelly, Brendan, 160
Kerm, Patricia, 46–7
Killanin, Lord, 172
Kilmacurragh, Co Wicklow, 9
Kinsella, John, 71
Klein, Jacques, 178

Klimov, Valery, 173
Knappertsbusch, Hans, 10
Knowles, Gregory, 137
König, Gustav, 39
Kontarsky, Aloys, 107–8
Kosler, Zdenek, 136
Kürtz, Efrem, 43

L

Laing, David, 113
Lane, Joseph, 82
Lane, Robert, 127
Lange, Aloysia, 166–7
Lanigan, Cáit, 117
Larchet, J F, 24, 78
late-comers, 44
Leeming, Miss, 97
Leeson, Victor, 74, 76, 125, 140
Leigh, Adèle, 47
Lemass, Seán, 154, 157, 158
Lentin, Louis, 175, 177
Lewis, Vic and his Orchestra, 40
Liberace, 36–8
light music, 37–8
lighting, concert, 61, 138, 146, 163
Lillis, David, 71, 73–4
Limerick, 175
Lindsay Singers, 125
Lisenbee, Thomas, 72
Little, Carol (later Acton), 10
live performance, 165
Lombard and Ulster Banking, Ireland, 172, 175
London, Westminster Abbey, 97
London Symphony Orchestra, 149
Loriod, Jeanne, 131
Loriod, Yvonne, 131, 132
Los Angeles, Victoria de, 62–3
Los Angeles Chamber Orchestra, 72
Louafi, Alan, 163
Lower Fitzwilliam Street, Dublin, 95
Lurçat, Jean, 132
Lynch, Joe, 74

M

Maazel, Lorin, 143, 144, 176
Maggio Musicale, Florence, 20
Magidoff, Robert, 42
Maguire, Hugh, 145
Mahler, Gustav: Symphony no 3, 168–9
Mainz, 140
Makower, Anne, 127
Malirsh, Victor, 122, 139
Marshall, Rhona, 177
Mascagni, Pietro, 17
Masonic Hall, Dublin, 139
Mazzoli, Ferruccio, 54
McBrien, Peter, 125
McGrath, Mabel, 125
McGrath, Raymond, 156
McNamara, Brian, 129–30
McSwiney, Veronica, 74
Meadmore, Norman, 81
medieval music, 123–4
Mee, Liam, 74
Mellerick, Capt, 78
Mendelssohn, Felix, 79; Elijah, 125–6; Midsummer Night's Dream, 88
Menotti, Gian Carlo, 17
Menuhin, Hephzibah, 61
Menuhin, Yehudi, 13, 42–4
Messiaen, Oliver, 13; *Turangalîla* symphony, 130–2, 163
Meulien, Maurice, 150
Miller, Kevin, 46
Miller, Niven, 46
Milne, David, 123
Milne, John, 123, 124
misprints, 98–9
Monte Carlo, National Orchestra of, 58
Monteverdi, Claudio, 116; Orfeo, 126–8
mood: critical, 29
Moore, Gerald, 62, 63, 111
Moran, Lona, 127

Morris, Hazel, 117
Morrison, Harry, 53
Moscow Chamber Orchestra, 122
Mozart, Wolfgang Amadeus, 108, 142; Divertimento in E flat, 108; *Don Giovanni; Idomeneo,* 167; Marriage of Figaro, 46–7; Musical Joke, 73–4; Piano concerto no 15, 61–2; Piano sonata no 8, 165; Piano sonata no 9, 64; Piano sonata no 11, 111; Slow preludes with transcriptions of fugues, 108; Symphony no 29, 72–3, 167, 175; Symphony no 33, 167; Symphony no 41, 'Jupiter,' 61
Mozart style, 166
Munch, Charles, 27, 35
Murphy, Suzanne, 166–7
music: community of, 26; state sponsorship, 116
Music Association of Ireland, 13, 56, 57, 152
music theatre, 137–8
Musical Times, The, 13
Mussorgsky, Modest: Pictures at an Exhibition, 114, 129, 174–5
Myers, Norman, 33

N

na Gopaleen, Myles, 94
Natali, Valiano, 54
National Concert Hall: acoustic, 176; campaign for, 12, 13, 94, 151–9; opening, 159–61; performances, 149, 162, 164, 166, 168, 169, 172, 174, 175, 177
National Symphony Orchestra, 45
Neeson, Geraldine, 140
New Irish Chamber Orchestra, 122–3, 126, 139, 142, 166, 167
NICO, *see* New Irish Chamber Orchestra
Nilsson, Birgit, 51

Nin, Joaquin, 63
Nisbett, Margaret, 46
Nofri, Bruno, 53
nondescript performance, 29
Novakowski, Marian, 45

O

O'Brien, Oliver, 58
O'Boyle, Alice, 8
O'Connor, Catherine, 82
O'Connor, Terry, 81
O'Conor, John, 110–12, 136, 177–9
O'Doherty, Michael, 159
O'Donovan, Fred, 159, 175
Ó Gallchóir, Andreas, 160
Ogdon, John, 64
O'Grady, Geraldine, 74
O'Kelly, Bill, 145
old age pensioners, 102–3
Olympia Theatre, Dublin, 62, 64
Ondes Martenot, 131–2
opera: as theatre, 127
opinion: criticism as, 15–17
orchestras: size, 61; soul, 93
O'Reilly, Alpho, 175
Ó Riada, Seán: Hoelderlin songs, 160
Orlandini, Evaristo, 54
O'Rourke, Pádraig, 128
O'Shea, Marie, 133, 134
O'Shea, Milo, 74
O'Suilleabháin, Tomás, 117
O'Sullivan, Eilís, 117
Our Lady's Choral Society, 44, 58–9, 78, 135
Oxford Companion to Music (Scholes), 25

P

Palestine, 10
Panufnik, Andrzej, 13, *104*
Paravicini, Professor, 53
Park Singers, 170

Patterson, Frank, 122, 138, 139
Paul, Tibor, 61, 62, 65, 66, 70, 78, 81, 88–91, 151
Pavarotti, Luciano, 145–7
Pearce, Colman, 160, 161, 168, 169, 170, 171, 176
Pease, James, 46
performance: nondescript, 29
performers, *see* artists
Periquet, 57
personal pronoun: used in criticism, 16–17
personality,: singer's, 62
Petrarch, 146
Philharmonia Orchestra, 43
Philharmonic Society of London, 79
Phoenix Hall, Dublin, 20, 26, 135, 151
political correctness, 102–3
pop music, international, 120–1
Porter, W.B., *92*
Potter, A.J., 10–11
praise: finely-tailored, 28–9; unmerited, 21–2
Prieur, André, 122, 142
Proctor's Tripod Harvesting Ltd, 10
programming, 43
Prokofiev, Sergei: Classical symphony, 173; Piano sonata no 6, 64; Violin sonata in D, 55
Prout, Ebenezer: Duet Concertante for Harmonium, 74
Puccini, Giacomo: *Manon Lescaut*, 147; *Turandot*, 53–4, 147
Purcell, Henry, 118
Purcell, Lucienne, 123, 124

Q

quartet-playing, 20

R

Radio Éireann, 17, 69, 153
Radio Éireann Choral Society, 69

Radio Éireann Light Orchestra, 38
Radio Éireann Music Festival: 69
Radio Éireann Singers, 69
Radio Éireann Symphony Orchestra (later RTÉSO), 18, 38–9, 41, 45, 47, 62, 66, 69, 70, 71, 81, 151
Radio Telefís Éireann, 140, 175; Acton on, 12, 13; music programmes, 90
Radio Telefís Éireann Academica String Quartet, 140–1
Radio Telefís Éireann Chorus, 160
Radio Telefís Éireann Singers, 160
Radio Telefís Éireann Symphony Orchestra, 45, 88–91, 129, 131, 135, 162, 163; home for, 151, 158
Railton, Dame Ruth, 147
Rainier, Prince, of Monaco, 59
Rathmines and Rathgar Musical Society, 81–2
Ravel, Maurice, 63, 129
RDS, *see* Royal Dublin Society
readers: critic's repsonsibility towards, 17–18, 21
Reagan, Ronald, 170
record reviews, 13
recorded performance, 165
Reddin, Jeannie, 56
Renaissance music, 114–17
renaissance music, 123–4
Rex, Al, 40
Richter, Sviatoslav, 112–14
Rinaldi, Margherita, 146
Robinson, Andrew, 123
Robinson, George, 38
Robinson, Jennifer, 123, 139
rock 'n' roll, 40–1
Rodrigo, Joaquin, 63
Roe, Olwen, 33
Rosen, Albert, 131
Rosen, Charles, 112
Rostropovich, Mstislav, 80–1, 84
Roth, Edward, 90

Royal Dublin Society, 27, 113, 134, 135, 143, 147, 150, 164, 171, 178; acoustic, 135, 149; audiences, 26; programme, 20; 250th anniversary, 149
Royal Hibernian Hotel, Dublin, 56
Royal Irish Academy of Music, 10, 13
RTE Guide, 140
RTÉSO, *see* Radio-Telefís Éireann Symphony Orchestra
Rubinstein, Arthur, 85–6
Rugby School, 9–10
Rupert Guinness Hall, Dublin, 75
Russell, Anna, 87

S

Saint-Saens, Camille, 74
St Ann's church, Dublin, 138, 147
St Francis Xavier Hall, Dublin, 88, 129
St James's Gate Musical Society, 76
St Patrick's Cathedral, Dublin, 65, 122, 142; choir, 65, 160
St Sepulchre's Consort, 123–4
Salzburg Festival, 20
Sandford, Irene, 89, 126, 138–9
Sargent, Sir Malcolm, 34–5
Sauerzweig, Herr, 77
Sawallisch, Wolfgang, 52, 60
Scarlatti, Alessandro, 63
Schoenberg, Arnold: Chamber symphony, 137; *Pelléas und Mélisande*, 131
Scholes, Percy, 25
Schubert, Franz: *Ave Maria*, 137; Piano sonata no 10, 165; Quartet no 10, 171; Songs, 63; Symphony no 9, 60
Schumann, Robert, *Frauenliebe und Leben* 56, 57; Fantasy in C, 165–6; Songs, 118
Score,The, 17

Scottish Opera, 118
Seán O'Boyle award, 8, 13
Searson, Betty, 135
Seeber, Helmut, 139
Seeger, Pete, 83
Segovia, Andrès, 32
'senior citizen': use of term, 102–3
Sestetto Luca Marenzio, 116
Shacklock, Constance, 45
Shawe-Taylor, Desmond, 109
Sheridan, Mary, 133
Shostakovich, Dmitri: Chamber symphony, 122; Quartet no 1 in C, 75
Sibelius, Jean: Symphony no 1, 150
Siercke, Alfred, 39
Silvestri, conductor, 90
Sirbu-Danciła, Mariana, 140
Smetana, Bedrich: Quartet no 1 'From my Life,' 171
Smetana Quartet, 80, 107, 171–2
Smith, Alan, 159
Smith, Gillian, 139
soloists, in chamber groups, 107
song titles, erroneous, 99
Spence, Sir Basil, 95
Stamitz, Johann, 142
standards, critical, 18–22, 100, 106–7
standing ovations, 177–8
Stanford, C V, 97–8
Staveley, Colin, 133
Stern, Isaac, 22, 55–6, 80
Stockhausen, Karlheinz: *Inori*, 162–4; piano music, 108–10; *Sirius*, 164
Stockhausen, Markus, 164
Strauss, Johann II: *Fledermaus, Die*, 176–7
Strauss, Richard, 10, 90; *Also Sprach Zarathustra*, 131; *Heldenleben, Ein*, 131; Tone Poem, Don Juan, 34, 35, 70

Stravinsky, Igor, 67–9, 177; *Baiser de la fée, Le*, 67–8; Chorale variations on Bach's *Von Himmel hoch*, 68; Firebird suite, 176; *Sacre du Printemps, Le*, 61, 62; Symphony of psalms, 68–9
string players, Czech, 135–6
Sullivan, Betty, 139
Sullivan, Sir Arthur: Mikado, The, 81
Svetlanov, Yevgeny, 172
Sweeney, Eric, 127, 128
Sweeney, Peter, 123, 124
Sweeney, Vanessa, 123, 124
Swieten, Gottfried, Baron van, 108

T

'Table for Two,' 13
Tchaikowsky, Peter Illitch, 68; Symphony no 6, 81, 173; Violin Concerto in D, 129–30
Testore Quartet, 133
theatre: opera as, 127
Theatre Royal, Dublin, 12, 32, 36, 40, 41, 43, 55, 58, 151; demolition, 134
Third Day Chorale, 133
Thomas, Mary, 137, 138
Thompson, Randall, 97
Thompson, Sam, 125
Three Choirs Festival (1932), 10
Tierney, Roderick, 82
Toscanini, Arturo, 10
Tosti, Sir Paolo: Songs, 146
Treptow, Günther, 39
Trinity College, Cambridge, 10
Trinity College, Dublin, 32, 71, 115, 123
Trio Italiano D'Archi, 107–8
Troy, Dermot, 58
Tryon, Valerie, 96
Turnbull, Alicia, 33
Turner, Eva, 54
Twomey, Violet, 138, 139, 160

U

Udovick, Lucilla, 54
unemployed, the, 103
University College, Dublin, 158
University of Dublin Choral
  Society, 32–4
'unwaged, the,' 103
USSR Symphony Orchestra, 172–3

V

variety artists, 37–8
Varsity Weekly, 10
Vaughan Williams, Ralph, 98;
  Poisoned Kiss, 10
Verdi, Giuseppe: *Traviata, La*, 144
Vezzosi, Ernesto, 54
Victoria, Queen of England, 79
Victory, Gerard, 159; Improbable
  Prelude, 73
Vienna Philharmonic Orchestra,
  35, 36, 175–7
Villa-Lobos, Heitor, 32
Virtuosi di Roma, 72
Vitali, Giovanni Battista:
  Chaconne, 55
Vito, Gioconda da, 151
Vivaldi, Antonio, 71; Four
  Seasons, 123
Vives, Amadeo, 63

W

Wagner, Richard, 49; *Tristan und
  Isolde*, 48, 50–2; *Walküre, Die*,
  38–9
Wagner, Wieland, 39
Wagner, Wolfgang, 48, 50, 51
Waibel, Xavier, 39
Walker, Ralph, 33
Walsh, Caroline, 159
Walsh, Dr Tom, 92
Walton, William: Overture,
  Portsmouth Point, 150

Waters, George, 159
Webern, Anton, 68, 137
Weimar Germany, 50
Weiss, Silvius Leopold, 32
Welsh National Opera, 166
West, Christopher, 47
Wexford, 71
Wexford Opera, 47
Wexford Opera Festival, 10–11, 13,
  144
White, Jack, 11
Williams, Douglas, 133
Williamson, Billy, 40
Wilson, Margaret, 124
Wilson, Thomas, 128
Windgassen, Wolfgang, 51
Wustman, John, 147
Wyse, Pearse, 158

Y

Yansons, Arvid, 172, 173
Yeats, Gráinne, 117
Yeats, Jack, 132
Young, Alexander, 58
Young, William, 133, 138, 139,
  160
Ypres, Battle of (1916), 9

Z

Zakin, Alexander, 55